SURFACE
TENSIONS

SURFACE
TENSIONS

Searching for Sacred Connection
in a Media-Saturated World

For Jacob—
Hopefully you'll understand my
weirdness more after reading. 😉
Love, Nathan Roberts

NATHAN ROBERTS

Surface Tensions: Searching for Sacred Connection
in a Media-Saturated World

Hendrickson Publishers Marketing, LLC
P. O. Box 3473
Peabody, Massachusetts 01961-3473

ISBN 978-1-61970-766-5

Photographs used on chapter pages with the generous permission of the photographers: chapter two photograph by Mary Rempel, chapter three photograph by Laura Kreuger, chapter five photograph by Sherry Webster Klein, and chapter six photograph by Louisa Raitt.

Printed in the United States of America

First Printing — July 2016

Library of Congress Cataloging-in-Publication Data

A catalog record for this book is available from the Library of Congress.
Hendrickson Publishers Marketing, LLC ISBN 978-1-61970-766-5

To my parents, Mark and Linda Roberts, for supporting my creativity with boundless commitment. If it weren't for the table you gave me, I wouldn't draw at all.

CONTENTS

FOREWORD

I TEACH the topic and write for the Internet, but I rarely like books on media. Their insights usually feel tired by the time they get to print, existing somewhere between the most obvious of epiphanies and "get off my lawn" grumpiness. The kids these days, with their iGoogles and their Tweet-Flix and their hot takes—they're getting dumber and less thoughtful, right?

Leave it to a true Millennial to set the record straight. I've known Nate since he started his undergraduate work at NYU, and I always knew he was a smart, thoughtful guy. He read books and philosophy and stared at a lot of screens, studying movies. But I didn't realize the half of it. And I was delighted to encounter him on the pages of this book.

Surface Tensions is a wonderfully allusive name for what works equally well as a small primer on media and a memoir of growing up in a thoroughly mediated age. That means all kinds of things. My favorite media theorist, Tom de Zengotita—with whom I studied in graduate school, coincidentally also at NYU—wrote a whole book on the topic, *Mediated*. Drawing on people like Baudrillard and Heidegger, he writes about how part of living in the twenty-first century is experiencing "reality" as a blunted thing, passed to us through a world that's catering to our particular whims. I didn't have to fend off a tiger or ford a river to get to work this morning. I just got on a bus, and I didn't have to stand out in the cold wondering when the bus was coming, because the transit authority in New York City has a number I can text for that information. I'm writing this on a computer on which the trackpad is specifically calibrated to my touch. My Twitter feed keeps alerting me to new posts, all from people I chose to follow, people who don't annoy or frustrate me, people I find interesting. (Sometimes I forget this, assuming that reality mirrors my feed. Then I go read the comments section on any article on the Internet.)

The best example of this I know comes from a movie: *Wall-E*, Pixar's story of a robot who got left on earth when the humans departed, their rampant consumerism having rendered the planet uninhabitable because of all the disposable crap. The movie is a true achievement in cinema (the first forty minutes or so are riveting and, essentially, silent). But it's when Wall-E hitches a ride up to the space station housing all the humans that things really get interesting.

Having left the dirty reality of their apparently dying planet, the humans have constructed a reality that requires them to interact only with screens. They talk to one another through screens. They sit in hovering lounge chairs and move about the ship, sipping their meals from giant cups with straws and hitting buttons to change the color of their pajama-like clothing. Everything is soft and candy-colored, designed by a corporation for their maximum comfort. Tiny robots mill about the ship, cleaning up and making sure nobody encounters any difficulty. No standing is necessary, and so the humans' muscles have atrophied, rendering them basically as blobs with (atrophying) brains.

Into this strange world comes Wall-E, a robot with rust and a personality. Early on, he bumps a human, causing her to both look at him askance and snap out of her mediated existence. She meets a person—face to face, not through a screen—and soon, all the humans on the ship are forced to encounter one another without all the rough edges smoothed off. That encounter with one another helps them realize how to save their race, and maybe even save their planet. All because a little robot got a bit messy and knocked them off balance.

I'm not sure he'll take it as a flattering comparison, but I think Nate is emulating Wall-E in these pages. Sometimes he is reflecting on the difficulty of connection, on how the devices we use connect us to (or disconnect us from) others. He does that as a digital native, a person who accepts that we can't just go live on a hill in Kentucky and pretend the outside world doesn't exist. We Christians are called to faithfully live in *the world that is,* a world of screens and recordings and text messages. Nate's honesty, humor, and insight help us see how that might be accomplished.

But he does something else, too, which is to shake up our encounters with God, which in twenty-first century America are so often mediated through the truisms and tired clichés we've been leaning on for years, the assumptions about what it looks like to "be Christian." A pastor's kid is just the right person to challenge that idea. He isn't trying to reinvent the church or make faith more "relevant"—he just shows us an insider's perspective on growing beyond a mediated faith and into a real faith, a true encounter with God and the one Mediator, Jesus. And he thinks that can only happen as we encounter one another in real ways, whether or not devices and movies and music are involved.

You'll be encountering Nate's story through another medium—the ink and paper of a book (or perhaps the screen of your e-reader)—but I hope you'll sense the real presence behind these pages. I'm glad he's decided to share them with us. I hope it knocks you off balance, makes you laugh, and helps you yearn for a real encounter with living presence.

Alissa Wilkinson
Critic at Large, *Christianity Today*
Assistant Professor of English and Humanities,
The King's College
February 4, 2016
New York City

ENTERTAINING MEDIA

I'm entertained and I'm uncomfortable about it. We're near the end of *Gypsy,* performed by an all-star cast from my charter school, Orange County High School of the Arts. I'm in eighth grade, sitting next to my mom, watching a high school girl perform a striptease.

After a difficult, unsuccessful childhood on the vaudeville circuit, our timid heroine finally gets a chance to nab the spotlight and make her draconian stage mother proud—at a grimy burlesque joint in Wichita, Kansas, sometime during Great Depression.

Even after she's renamed Gypsy Rose Lee, our heroine has a rough go of it onstage. She's awkward, glacial, and more than a little weary of those leering, whistling gentlemen in the dark. When she paces back and forth, Gypsy looks more like a child waiting to use the bathroom than an object of desire. Some presumably mustachioed sleazeball catcalls: "Show us some skin!" (The scene is staged so that *we,* the audience, are treated like stand-ins for those fine gentlemen. Keep in mind that I'm a budding pubescent sitting next to my mother. There's a reason I remember this so vividly.)

Gypsy doesn't stay aloof for long, though. This scene transforms into a montage. The production uses every fade-out-fade-in to fly through time and crank up the dial. She begins to strut around, swinging her hips like an ever-widening pendulum. Sequins grow flashier and flashier as outfits shrink smaller and smaller. Gypsy addresses the audience: poking, prodding, tantalizing the poor gentlemen before belting a slowed-down, sleazed-up version of the same refrain we've heard her perform her whole life long. The lyrics, obnoxious but harmless when screeched by a wannabe child star in Act One, pick up a couple extra coats of smut:

Let me entertain you
Let me make you smile
Let me do a few tricks
Some old and then some new tricks
I'm very versatile
And if you're real good
I'll make you feel good
I want your spirits to climb
So let me entertain you
And we'll have a real good time, yes sir.
We'll have a real good time.[1]

It's no wonder the word "entertain" made me cringe for such a long time after this.

Due to some combination of period authenticity and child pornography laws, there was no actual nudity in that production, fortunately. And *Gypsy*, despite its cynical bite, generally reconfirms any conservative's worst fears about secular entertainment. Under that show's cruel gaze, the entertainment industry is one big seduction factory, calibrated to lure you onto its assembly line, push you down a slippery slope and shove you into an underworld of ambition, tyranny, vanity, compromise, and self-loathing. *Gypsy* is a spectacularly entertaining piece of anti-entertainment. It chimes in with the author Michael Chabon when he claims that entertainment

> wears spandex, pasties, a leisure suit studded with blinking lights. . . . It engages regions of the brain far from the centers of discernment, critical thinking, ontological speculation. It skirts

the black heart of life and drowns life's lambency in a halogen glare. . . . Entertainment, in short, means junk, and too much junk is bad for you—bad for your heart, your arteries, your mind, your soul.[2]

I didn't know this Chabon quote back then, but as I montaged through middle school and high school, I began thinking Chabon-like thoughts. I loved movies, but whenever a peer said something like: "*Transformers 2* wasn't, you know, Oscar-worthy, but come *on*, it *was* entertaining," I felt the Gypsy's ghost rattle around inside.

And if you're real good, I'll make you feel good, I want your spirits to climb. . . .

It was, in fact, this very gut reaction that led me to find Chabon's essay on entertainment, "The Pleasure Principle," so surprising and significant in 2012.* By 2012, I had already abandoned all serious hope I ever placed in entertainment— the term and everything it stood for. So I nodded along as Chabon wrote: "serious people learn to mistrust and even revile" entertainment. I was with him as he laid out his fabulous lists, likening entertainment to "the fake-butter miasma of a movie-house lobby   karaoke and Jagermeister, Jerry Bruckheimer movies, a 'Street Fighter' machine grunting solipsistically in a corner of an ice-rink arcade."

But then he took me by surprise. He started to switch gears: "Maybe the reason for the junkiness of so much of what pretends to entertain us is that we have accepted—indeed, we have helped to articulate—such a narrow, debased concept of entertainment."

---

*I discovered the essay as a little hyperlinked blip on a blog post by the culture writer Alissa Wilkinson, who has since written a lovely essay about it for Fuller Theological Seminary's Brehm Center. I recommend it highly.

Wait . . . Really? What was I missing?

> The original sense of the word "entertainment" is a lovely one of
> mutual support through intertwining, like a pair of trees grown
> together, interwoven, each sustaining and bearing up the other.
> It suggests a kind of midair transfer of strength, contact across
> a void. . . . Derived senses of fruitful exchange, of reciprocal
> sustenance, of welcome offered, of grasp and interrelationship,
> of a slender span of bilateral attention along which things are
> given and received, still animate the word in its verb form: we
> entertain visitors, guests, ideas, prospects, theories, doubts and
> grudges. . . . [But] at some point in its history, the idea of en-
> tertainment lost its sense of mutuality, of exchange. One either
> entertains or is entertained, is the actor or the fan.

I had never entertained this "original sense," nor the interpersonal use we continually put it to. I felt as if this definition
had been sitting under my nose for a long time and I never
cared to sniff. As Chabon describes it, "entertainment" isn't
merely a term worth keeping around. It's a term that describes
the goal of *any* interpersonal activity. Isn't this the point of
life together, "midair transfer[s] of strength, contact across
a void," giving "reciprocal sustenance," cultivating "bilateral
attention along which things are given and received"? In his
popular 1939 book *Life Together*, Dietrich Bonhoeffer writes:
"Bearing means forbearing and sustaining. . . . The Christian
. . . must bear the burden of a brother. He must suffer and en-
dure the brother. . . . To bear the burden of the other person
means involvement with the created reality of the other, to ac-
cept and affirm it, and, in bearing with it, to break through to
the point where we take joy in it."[3] Every time the word "bear"
shows up in that quote, replace it with "entertain." Backed
by Chabon's definition, you'll end up with two semantically
similar statements.

I think about Chabon's essay a lot—not only because he unexpectedly resurrects a word I had prematurely crucified, but because he so aptly describes the two-pronged nature of human rapport while he's at it. We often underrepresent this covalent network in everyday speech. We stare, with tunnel vision, at either side of the equation: focusing exclusively on lover or beloved, attacker or victim, powerful or oppressed, actor or reactor. It's harder to entertain the notion of, say, beloved-lovers, even though we all want to be them ourselves.* It's hard to think about this network in the same way that it's hard to think about both sides of any multivariable equation. Bilateral relationships require bilateral attention.

But I think it's hard for another reason, too: there are always these *things* between us, far more complicated than an equation's equal sign. And in order to talk about them, I think we need to dust off another word tarnished by overuse.

That word is "media."

If we all collectively groan at the mention of "media"— and of course we do—that gives us all the more reason to save the term from further denigration. The word never did us any harm. "Media" was originally derived from the Latin word "medium," meaning "middle, center, midst, intermediate course, intermediary."

"Medium" carried these associations into English. For centuries, it has referred to "something which is intermediate between two degrees, amounts, qualities, or classes; a middle state," "a person or thing which acts as a mediary," "an intervening substance through which a force acts on objects at a distance."[4] I think we've mostly preserved these definitions,

---

* In messed up relationships, we also turn into victim-attackers. Perhaps the Israelis and the Palestinians ought to add this hyphenated word to their wheelhouse.

even if the only mediums around loiter in their little Lower East Side shops, luring gullible customers in with tarot cards, crystal balls, and mood lighting.

"Media," on the other hand, only maintains its original dignity as a smart-sounding Latin throwback: *en media res,* or, "in the middle of things." In the early twentieth century (1923, according to my trusty OED), media began to designate the "main means of mass communication, *esp.* newspapers, radio, and television." It's this new face of media, often called "the media," that gets us so riled up.

I Google search "quotes about media" and land on brainyquote.com. Everyone seems to be throwing hyperboles around. Malcolm X: "The media's the most powerful entity on earth. . . . Because they control the minds of the masses." JR, the Banksy-like street artist: "The more social media we have, the more we think we're connecting, yet we are really disconnecting from each other." Allen Ginsberg: "Whoever controls the media, the images, controls the culture." Amy Jo Martin: "Social Media is the ultimate equalizer." Jim Morrison: "Whoever controls the media, controls the mind." Mark McKinnon: "Technology and social media have brought power back to the people."[5] I could go on, but you know what I'm talking about. Depending on the person speaking, media either points to the decline of Western civilization or the dawn of a bright cultural future; totalitarian hegemony or democratic plurality; communicative efficiency or relational disaster.

I don't want to give the impression that this twentieth-century adaptation of "media" is inherently terrible. It's not. It's a clever way to pluralize the word "medium" and it was probably marshaled when somebody thought: *How in the world do we classify all of these new mediums?* But modern usage does make it tempting to treat "The Media" as some looming, singular deity (a good God or an evil God, take your pick), rather than various mediums, several "intervening sub-stances" caught in the same terminological net.

It's easy to think about "The Media" as a concrete entity that will either oppress or liberate you; it's much harder to think about many mediums. Mediums are, by their very nature, indeterminate. They're contingent spaces. The author Zadie Smith voices our communal angst when she cries:

> How persistent this horror of the middling spot is, this dread of the interim place! It extends through the specter of the tragic mulatto, to the plight of the transsexual, to our present anxiety—disguised as genteel concern—for the contemporary immigrant, tragically split, we are sure, between worlds, ideas, cultures, voices—whatever will become of them?[6]

In Protestant circles, we tend to ease our anxieties by resorting to polarities. We speak of sin: total disconnect between God and Man and Woman, manifest in the eternal reality of Hell. And then we do a full 180-degree turn. We look toward and yearn for the fruit of salvation: unmediated, communal intimacy with God and Man and Woman. While these polarities can bring spiritual reality into sharp focus (Flannery O'Connor: "To the hard of hearing you shout, and for the almost blind you draw large and startling figures"), they can also make it harder to cast a cold eye on the contingent spaces where we experience both communion and divorce, relation and isolation, unity and discord—and often a little bit of all that simultaneously. It's much easier to gesture toward the solved and unsolved equations, and decry the dangers of moral relativism, than it is to engage complex ethical problems *en media res*.

Yet for some reason, I have spent my whole life attracted to media, in all senses of the word. As a so-called Millennial, I have grown into what the pundits call an "increasingly media-saturated culture." I have matured alongside television, video cassette players, personal computers, cell phones, laptops, blogs, iPhones, MySpace, Facebook, Twitter, Snapchat, and so on. I've witnessed that interpersonal modifier, "social," welded onto "media" like a bright, new, sequined outfit. And I've engaged with it all like a kid at a strange, ever-evolving candy shop.

But this is just the tip of the iceberg. I've spent my life attracted to so *many* things that rest between us: drawings, stories, movies, paintings, comedy, literature, musical theater, and so on. And more often than not, I'm embarrassed to say, I've been more invested in the things that rest between us than the very notion of *us*. I reluctantly agree with Phillip Lopate, a fellow cinephile, when he says: "I would not argue either if someone wanted to maintain that chronic moviegoing often promotes a passivity before life, a detached tendency to aestheticize reality, and, I suppose, a narcissistic absorption that makes it harder to contact others."[7] The twenty-two year old guy writing a memoir, *narcissistically absorbed*?! Your Honor, I plead the fifth.

Of course, the dark cloud of solipsism hovers over my head, just as it does for many writers. And yet, I hear Chabon's (and, for that matter, Bonhoeffer's, and maybe even the Holy Spirit's) soft, encouraging voice remind me:

> entertainment—as I define it, pleasure and all—remains the only sure means we have of bridging, or at least of feeling as if we have bridged, the gulf of consciousness that separates each of us from everybody else. The best response to those who would cheapen and exploit it is not to disparage or repudiate but to reclaim entertainment as a job fit for artists and for audiences, a two-way exchange of attention, experience and the universal hunger for connection.

This memoir, not unlike *Gypsy*, will entertain the very notion of entertainment. These pieces of paper—whether glued together or distilled into zeros and ones and shot into dynamic graphical outputs—are made to bridge the gulf of consciousness that separates us. They're about the bridges I've spent my whole life glued to. They're about the means by which we try, and often fail, to entertain each other. They're about the media that rests between us—social, antisocial, everything in-between. And skirting around the edges of this book, and all around us, I dare suggest, is the shape of a God who, though seemingly set apart from us by the gulf of time and space, sensed "through a glass, darkly," may be the very medium by which we connect.

Let me entertain you. We'll have a real good time.

PART ONE

Anxiety comes **from the self** as ultimate concern, from the fact that the self cannot bear this ultimate concern: it buckles and wavers under the strain, and eventually, inevitably, it breaks.

Christian Wiman, *My Bright Abyss*

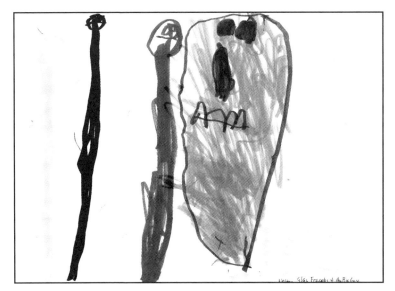

Fraggles and The Big Guy, September, 1996

CHAPTER 1

SPECTACLE

A CROWD holds a torchlight vigil in holy silence. It stands in a wide circle around a small, leafy tree. Two children, Dario and Maria, have witnessed a miracle here. They've seen the Virgin Mary. Her feet didn't even touch the ground.

Suddenly, generators growl and spotlights shine and media men glide their camera cranes up as a bellowing crowd pours into the clearing. Dario and Maria lead the way. He wears a raincoat and she wears a white, frilly dress. They're repeatedly shot by their boisterous disciples—cameramen, all of them, sprinting and dodging and ducking for the best possible photograph. They kneel in front of the tree. A film director runs up to Maria—"How are you, sweetie?"—and shouts up to his cinematographer: "Focus on them with the crowd behind! It's dark back here!" The flashbulbs snap and the sick lie on stretchers and the reverent pray, waiting for God knows what.

The crowd begins to push on the police blockade, crying: "Heal me!" Dario and Maria's grandparents, kneeling inside the circle, nod approvingly.

A lightbulb explodes. Rain begins to pour. Umbrellas fly up. A far-off woman wails an Italian aria. Dario and Maria are soaked. She speaks in his ear; he nods.

Maria turns around and points: "The Madonna's over there!" She trots off and kneels again. He follows. The crowd pushes in harder, cries harder. It rains harder. The photographers fall on their hands and knees, cameras flashing. The blockade is breached! The kids run another way, chased by the wailing, flailing horde. Then—"There she is!"—yet another, swarmed by grunting, whistling, singing, sprinting, shouting.

Their uncle breaks through—"They'll catch pneumonia in this rain!"—and lifts Maria in his arms. He appeals to the mob: "Quiet! The Madonna said to build a church here or she won't appear anymore. Goodnight! Go home!" He's met with shouts of indignation. He takes off with the children. The mob charges after him, stretchers in hand. A headscarfed woman runs to the fragile tree and starts stripping branches. Others follows suit, grasping, yanking, shrieking in the pounding rain. The tree writhes, flails, hits the ground and the crowd keeps pulling. A woman attacks Paparazzo, a cameraman: "How dare you act like that! You're worse than hyenas! You have no respect for anyone!" Engines ignite. Cars honk honk *honk, hooonkkk!*

"He's dead!" A large truck literally quakes in the wind. "He's dead!" Dario's grandmother wanders aimlessly with hands on her face like Munch's screamer. She leans on the quaking truck. And sure enough, she's right—the scaffolding still stands, the spotlights still stand, but the evening's faithful dreamers are replaced with a bright morning's mourners. A priest leans over the boy on the stretcher, closes the child's eyes, makes a cross on his forehead with his thumb and covers his head with a bright white sheet. Paparazzo crosses himself and takes a photograph.

I saw this scene from Federico Fellini's 1959 classic *La Dolce Vita* for the first time last night at the Brooklyn Academy of Music. I can't get it out of my mind. It's a terrifying, showboating sequence in a film full of showboating sequences. It's all the more pronounced because Marcello, the existentially conflicted tabloid journalist, watches chaos unfold from the sidelines. He joins with us, with Fellini, fretting as the gliding camera and the cacophonous soundscape and the morose denouement ask an ever-pressing question: *What in the world is media doing to our children?* Fellini's conclusion is dour. Personified at its very worst by the paparazzi (the term "paparazzi" is, in fact, derived from the film's tabloid photographer, Paparazzo), Fellini's media exploits children, surrounds them, chases them, and, ultimately, crushes them dead. What is lost in this brave new technological world, in the beautiful—my *goodness* is this movie beautiful—aestheticized mediascape?

Future generations are lost. In the next sequence, when Fellini's camera floats over to two chubby, backlit children, smiling mischievously, mouths agape, we fear that the image must be too good to be true. We're right to fear. These kids fare no better than Dario and Maria. *La Dolce Vita*'s media-driven determinism is deadly determinism.

But Fellini's media is mid-century, modernist media. Powerful moguls perpetuate the memory of Mussolini: Marcello's newspaper is described as "half-fascist"; paparazzi jog around like dedicated soldiers in pursuit. Fellini's vision of decadent, image-centric emptiness is ever compelling, ever intoxicating on the silver screen, but his media is media of the Studio System—the site of the "The Miracle Tree" looks like a Cecil B. DeMille set—of Adorno and Horkheimer's "Culture Industry," of Don Draper and propaganda and unbeatable conglomerates and white-toothed mouths drinking shiny glasses of Coke on big bright billboards. He had no vision (and how could he?) of a democratized web space, of personal blogs, personal computers, social media. In Fellini's vision, the media tramples over normal people and hollows out its complicit workers; in 2016, normal people generate content and threaten the livelihood of its complicit workers. Marcello's own job, so sexy in the 1960s, finds itself in danger.

But I think this scene stuck with me for another reason: it perceives the site of "divine revelation" as the site of a media spectacle. It is as if Guy Debord's famous Marxist tome *The Society of Spectacle*, published eight years after *La Dolce Vita*, was directly inspired by it. Modern society, Debord claims, "presents itself as an immense accumulation of spectacles. All that once was directly lived has become mere representation."[8] And the spectacle isn't just "a collection of images"—Dario and Maria and the Sacred Tree aren't *just* representative images on a television—it's "a social relationship between people that is mediated by images." The image of two children dressed up next to a lone tree in the wilderness mediates the whole wild social affair.

The spectacle is heightened—when the cameramen visit Dario and Maria's grandparents, both of them strike exaggerated poses: Grandma with her trembling arm out like George Washington crossing the Delaware, Grandpa on his knees, singing a spiritual ballad at the top of his lungs—scripted—a television reporter asks the Uncle a question and hands him a pre-written response—and commodified. When a priest is asked whether the miracle was real he replies: "Those children are lying. Seeing the Madonna changes a person. They don't try to profit from it. Miracles occur in prayer and silence, not in the middle of this hubbub." He says this even before the Sacred Tree is charged like Wal-Mart on Black Friday. Sacredness is imagined, longed for, needed—but never witnessed. Visual representation of the Sacred does not lead to a lived experience of the sacred.

I recognize this site. I spent my formative years in a similar place.

✶ ✶ ✶ ✶ ✶

When Dad told stories at parties, I would listen and yearn.

He was the senior pastor of Irvine Presbyterian Church and they were usually church parties. I yearned to master his sense of dramatic buildup and LOL-worthy release, to walk his tightrope between reverence and irreverence, to exude his self-confidence, to be admired and loved like he was admired and loved. Kids weren't finger-flinging "the world's angriest flock of furious feathered fowl" on their iPads back then, but when they chose to play Nintendo 64 or jump off the high, flat ledge into that spectacular Dietz-family-designed pool with its faux-natural rock walls and its "sea cave" and its seven waterfalls and its shiny slide and its underwater speakers,* I would pull up a mesh patio chair and sit with those middle-aged white guys instead.

Those congregants circled up in their Lacoste polos and their SoCal shorts while they drank red wine and listened

---

* We called this pool "Dietzyland." A high compliment, indeed: Disneyland was the spectacle Orange County aspired to be.

to Dad and laughed. I felt proud; I loved Dad and I loved that other people loved him. In his *Trouble In Paradise* review, Roger Ebert wrote that the film "is about people who are almost impossibly adult, in that fanciful movie way—so suave, cynical, sophisticated, smooth. . . . They glide." Those UC, USC, Ivy League-educated Orange County-ites, smart and cynical about culture and politics, too suave and sophisticated for the shenanigans of most atheists and Lefties, seemed almost impossibly adult in that fanciful Moving Image way. Almost impossible, too, seemed timid, quirky, artsy-kid Nathan's chance at becoming one of them, much less becoming their Pastoral Entertainer. But he wanted to glide. And he doesn't really want to admit it, but, deep down, part of him sometimes feels like he needs to—but can't really—glide.

Maybe not the *same* glide, though. Maybe those sorts of conversations now carry the slight scent of performance with them. Or maybe I've just heard Dad tell the same stories too many times. He keeps retelling them. The older he gets, the more he forgets how many times he's told them. Here's one I've heard a half-dozen times, at least:

I am a toddler. He's playing a toddler game with me.

"What does a dog say?"

"Woof."

"What does a cat say?"

"Meow."

"What does a mouse say?"

"Click."

He frowns: "No, Nathan, what does a mouse say?"

"Click!" I stick out my pointer finger and jab it downward. *The mouse clicks, right?*

That story always evokes little chuckles of surprise and recognition, chuckles that say: *Oh, of* course *he thought that! He's never known a world without personal computers!* I've always understood the basic thrust of the punch line: the ironic error-turned-accuracy, the linguistic reversal. But I didn't understand its deeper resonances until I started to grow up. Since I haven't lived without personal computers, I have no idea how strange the structural conditions of my life must seem to those raised computerless. Innocence cannot be reverse-engineered; I can try to imagine how things were before the mid-1980s, but it takes work—work I do best when I'm watching older films on my MacBook Air computer. The technological conditions that shape our young selves seem utterly natural. As my parents grew up, the telephone pole seemed as natural as the tree; for beta-Nathan, a computer seemed as natural as a living rodent—or even more natural in the green, sterile-clean suburbs of Irvine, California. When beta-Nathan was a toddler, he would carry around two types of security objects: yogurt cups and *Winnie the Pooh* videocassette tapes. Both were equally special, equally protective.

I only began to realize the significance of this anecdote when I sat in a borrowed church van. I was fifteen. My extended family, visiting Texas from California for the first time, sat in the back. I had my beloved camcorder strapped to my hand, ready to document some fresh, exciting memories, but we were stuck in Austin's unique kind of wrenching, senseless freeway traffic—no accidents, no construction, just *cars*. But my three-year-old cousin Brody sat in the back, utterly and endlessly fascinated with video cartoons on the iPhone he held five inches from his face. We were stuck in a drizzly, urban hellhole; our lives were helplessly determined by this metal hunk of twentieth-century tech and there he was: delighted by his own personal multiplex.

I was surprised. It didn't even occur to me that a child could *do* that. We tend to draw Platonic Ideal Childhoods from our wells of personal experience and chuck them onto other children (a move occasionally turned into art, successfully by Terrence Malick in *The Tree of Life*, a little less effectively by Richard Linklater in *Boyhood*). My Platonic Ideal Childhood had no room for watch-a-film-whenever-you-want type media technology. It seemed strange—unfair, too: how often did baby Nathan have to sit through mind-numbing Southern California traffic in his dreaded car seat, accompanied by scratchy cassette tapes of ladies singing in weird, exaggerated, "child-appropriate" tones? There seemed to be something wrong about this Austin scene, something inappropriately *privileged* about my cousin's golden ticket out of deadlock.*

And so, at age fifteen, before my childhood was even over, I began to grasp the surprised laughter that always followed my dad's anecdote. It came from busted picture of a Platonically Ideal Childhood. The Baby Boomers' Ideal Childhood featured mice that were, you know, squeaky *mice*. My Ideal Childhood featured unmitigated traffic. As the technologically-determined structure of the world changes more and more quickly, our generational normalcies begin to spread further and further apart. And so I felt my first twinge of stereotypical old man "When I was your age I had to walk to school ten miles in the snow barefoot" type feelings, made up of some combination of surprise and jealousy and insecurity and guilt and fear: how weird that childhood is changing so quickly; if only *I* could've had a cartoon-equipped iPhone when I was Brody's age; but wait, what is being *lost* as things change so quickly; what's *denuded*; what are we doing to these kids, changing the technological structure of their Platonically Ideal worlds?

---

* I didn't think, at the time, of how the iPhone spared us the pain of Brody's squirming and grasping and crying. We—my uncle Jay in particular, sitting next to him—were privileged by extension.

⋆ ⋆ ⋆ ⋆ ⋆

How to begin a memoir in an age when Facebook wants
to write our memoirs for us? Facebook used to give us "walls"
to write on, erected in the digital jungle just for us. Those
walls collected status updates and photographs and flirta-
tious pokes. But despite our moaning and the groaning and
the protest grouping, it forced us onto timelines in March
2012. Today, my Facebook timeline—vertically distributing
all of my wall stuff, plus so-called "life events," into two tidy
columns—scrolls down and down, past blurry pictures from
college parties, past embarrassingly confessional high school
statuses, past the summer day I joined Facebook in 2008 until
it hits December 21, 1992, the day beta-Nathan rolled out in
Newport Beach, California. "Born," my timeline proclaims.
It's into minimalism.

Birth was impressive before Facebook. "It all started out
when I was just a little molecule," I wrote in a story at age seven,
"I grew bigger and bigger and I came out of my mommy's belly
button! I was so surprised." It's less surprising now. I'm not a
very impressive-looking newborn, according to the timeline.
Right below "Born": a little blue cartoon baby with a white dia-
per and an oblong head, like the child of a Smurf and a clip art
alien. I'm crouching in an unnatural position—pooping, I suppose. Facebook got the head right (the "Roberts Five Head,"
my family calls our long foreheads) but it got the color wrong:
I was a yellow, jaundiced alien. When Facebook gets its way,
of course, I'll replace this automated cartoon with an actual
photograph of little yellow me, and, while I'm at it, fill in the
timeline gap between 1992 and 2008 with pictures and "life
events" from moments long past. Then, only then, my cyber-
spaced life, my digital memoir, will be complete, available for
all to see, and you won't have to pay zilch for this wordy thing.

Why the timeline? I sometimes wonder. The timeline wasn't just a practical creation; posts were ordered chronologically on our walls, too. It's not an organizational necessity. Older photographs already linger in my mom's big leather photo albums, carefully organized by date and event. Those red, green, maroon books, heavy as Torah scrolls, are like Holy Books to me—and isn't Facebook designed for the ephemeral thought, the delicious meal pic, the everyday conversation, the LOLs? I'd thought so. I'd like to think so.

But my timeline seems to have its mind set on the digitalization of life itself, from birth to death and even beyond the grave, when friends and family will share memories on my "memorialized account." We used to dream that we'd use technology to perpetuate our lived existence. It would heal our cancers and preserve our cryonically frozen bodies. Now our finite lives must perpetuate the existence of digital technology unto eternity as we offer up our denuded, aestheticized selves—photographically heightened, self-scripted, commodified for advertisers—one post at a time.

If we offer up our denuded, aestheticized selves, I should say. I don't plan to fill up my timeline any time soon. Facebook steals most of my day as it is; I'm that little blue iPhone app's slave, for all intents and purposes, but I won't let it win! I can even dredge up the philosopher Jacques Derrida for inspiration: "I have an impulse of fear or terror in the face of . . . a public space that makes no room for the secret. For me, the demand that everything be paraded in the public square and there be no internal forum is a glaring sign of the totalitarianization of democracy."[9] So, take that, Totalitarianism! In your face, Facebook! My timeline will remain defiantly incomplete. Maybe I'll post a gloating status update about it. Or add a new life event: "Defied Mark Zuckerberg."

It's all too easy to wax deterministic about the technological structures we're subjected to, about the timelines we're "forced" to adopt. This trap caught a whole slew of Marxists and Structuralists in the twentieth century, and a similar trap threatens to snare the wannabe prophets of the twenty-first—those who cry that the Internet is debilitating our intelligence and those who claim that we're nearing something like "The Singularity," an artificial-intelligence-aided paradise, "an era in which our intelligence will become increasingly nonbiological and trillions of times more powerful than it is today."[10]

I want to avoid that trap. It seems too dogmatic, too simple. But it wouldn't be so appealing if there weren't some sense behind its general intellectual thrust. I think even the most self-determined among us know that, at some deep level, our lives are radically mediated by forces beyond our control.

We've all been children, after all. We remember.

★ ★ ★ ★ ★

I see a flannelgraph, three-by-five. It's made for stuck-on paper Bible Story Guys, but it's empty in my mind's eye. The top half is bright blue. The bottom half is some variation of tan. The image is both heightened and suffocatingly restricted. It's as geometrically rigid as a Mondrian—just two boring flannel rectangles, one on top of another. If I stretch my imagination I see a few sand dune waves rounding out the tan square's top edge, but it still makes me shiver the way I shiver at Edward Hopper paintings: everything's too simple, too damn *empty*. Real life complications are too smoothed out, too mechanically stripped. This is an image of Sunday School.

If I Google image search "biblical flannelgraph," different images pop up, greener images. Perhaps flannelgraph storytelling has modernized, caught up with an era of iPads and flat screen TVs. (Yes, iPad flannelgraph apps exist—God provides.) Or perhaps I'm conflating whole varieties of tan, sand dune kid Bible products into this hair-raising image. It's not like the new flannelgraphs are much better, though: they imagine lush, impossibly lush, nearly neon green fields with full leafy trees and cool blue rivers. They're like nature preserves designed by Jeff Koons. They're pretty in the way that *Blue Velvet*'s opening shot is pretty. They're too pretty.

These are the images of Sunday School: didactic, simple, coloring book images. They're images that emerge when one of the strangest books ever compiled is stripped down to its bare, boring bones. They're wild, violent, metaphysical, sexually promiscuous stories commodified into moralistic scripts by Christian media companies, sold to churches, used by Sunday School teachers too embarrassed or worried-what-parents-will-say or—more often the not, in my lucky life, I think—amiably complicit to let the Bible's freak flag fly.

It feels like those Bible-mediating teachers mediated my entire childhood. Their flannelgraphs were interspersed with anarchic exceptions, of course: *Ben Hur*'s rip-roaring chariot race, rearing in front of my fifth grade Sunday School class on a sixty-two-inch flat screen in the Jack Davis Room; or the quirky, animated *Veggie Tales* vegetables goofing their way through clever riffs on Bible stories. But these images were so fun because they drew away from the dull source material, because they were exceptions to the rule. They didn't seem to take biblical gems and polish them until they shone; they didn't reveal innate quality. Like Damien Hirst's *For The Love of God* sculpture, they seemed to take old bones and pepper them with diamonds until they sparkled, spectacular. I loved Larry Boy, the talking cucumber superhero with

Super Suction Ears, but I had no idea what he was there to teach me.*

At the end of my flannelgraph days, as a budding seventh grader at a two-week-long summer camp, I sat before my counselor's light wood bunk bed. Yosemite Sierra Summer Camp became the rare Christian context in which I could be known as a simple individual, utterly unmediated by my obligatory Pastor's Kid identity. My cabin was supposed to hold a half-hour-long Bible study every morning, but we either used that time for goofy, leisurely Cabin Cleanups or more exciting things like planning music videos to film during Activity Time. I both enjoyed this Bible study skippage and felt little pricks of nagging guilt as if we were jumping straight to dessert. But as I sat beside the light wood bunk bed, Apache mentioned an "awesome" story. He *had* to read it to us. I couldn't recall hearing it before, so I sat, intrigued.

Although "Ehud Becomes Irael's Judge" is an inauspicious title, it did not disappoint: the Israelites were screwing things up again so the Lord handed Israel over to Eglon of Moab who was very not cool and—as seventh-grade Nathan would've put it—frickin' fat, and, so, after eighteen years, the Israelites asked God for help and God sent them a rescuer named Ehud who went to deliver tribute money to Eglon but kept a footlong, double-edged dagger strapped to his right thigh, which, after telling the king he had a "secret message"—effectively eliminating the presence of any meddling servants—he plunged into the king's belly where

---

*Now I'd say that an episode of *Veggie Tales* isolates the moral core of a Bible story and transmutes it and blows it up kid-size in a rather wonderful and brilliant way, but that's a complex narrative operation. Back then, those flights of fancy seemed more like flights of escape than flights of revelation.

it descended so deep that the handle disappeared into layers of viscous fat as the king filled his royal pantaloons before Ehud locked the doors and escaped *through a toilet.* In a cute little final twist, Ehud's servants found the doors locked but they assumed that the king must've been using the toilet because those emptied bowels smelled like death—which, in a delightful way, they literally did.

It's a story designed for middle school boys: secrecy, brutal violence, fat jokes and poop jokes all rolled into one. Stabbing a fatass, making him poop his pants, and escaping through a toilet? What's not to love? But even then, as I nodded along with my preteen brethren, I felt that there was something insufficient and shallow about this macabre tale. My parents didn't send me to *Game of Thrones* camp, after all. The shock-and-horror Bible seemed limited in its own unique, voyeuristic way.

And looking back now, I think it was just a bit too little, a little too late. Around this transitional period, with mom's help, I began collecting Christian media products in the hope that I could somehow make my faith my own: a green, hardcover devotional for teens (For teens! Sophisticated!); *Jesus Freaks,* with its real-world stories of brutally martyred Christian devotees (No-holds-barred violence! Sophisticated!); *How To Smell Like God,* with its true stories about sex and stuff; *Taming A Liger: Unexpected Spiritual Lessons From Napoleon Dynamite.* I couldn't sell the miracles to myself—my ganglia were already shaped by the tan, empty desert that still presses on my mind. It shaped my vision of Israel, of the whole Bible itself, to the extent that when eighteen-year-old Nathan had an actual opportunity to visit Israel his gut rejected the idea outright. Who would want to visit that barren wasteland, that empty, mind-numbing space of tans and browns, the land of pre-manufactured coloring books, of spoon-fed week-to-week boredom?

✳ ✳ ✳ ✳ ✳

Mom bought me a drawing table when I was three. It was long, white, rectangular, lined with red plastic, and nudged next to a dark, lacquered china cabinet in the corner of the dining room where bright white stripes of Southern California sun shot through venetian blinds.

I see myself sitting at that table. A white sheet of paper lies in front of me. It's the most vivid memory I have from those days because it's less of a memory than a feeling. I remember the uncontainable excitement I felt holding those big, fat, awkward Crayola markers in my hand. I remember adrenaline pumping blood to my fingertips, like Ehud ready to stab. I remember that white, boring rectangle, not forced on me like an empty flannelgraph, but *opened up for me*. And that's what I remember most: that feeling of infinite possibility, a world of absolute freedom inviting me in, prepared for my very hand, without laws or regulations or limitations.

But I didn't feel freedom in an abstract sense, exactly; I did not feel our conventional, Sartrean version of freedom of mere possibility, of "annihilating withdrawal," of a mental step back from the determined world. No, that's too simple. . . . I experienced a sort of glowing, perfect synthesis of possibility and necessity, an intoxicating weld of free will and determinism, a sense of utter possibility linked with the undeniable need to draw *something*, to extend myself on the sheet before me. And as mom reminds me, I drew and drew. All day, every day, whenever possible, I drew.

I looked, too. My favorite picture book location was the jungle. (Even the savannah, with its tan-brown grasslands, was a little too reminiscent of tan-brown Israel for my taste. The Old West, even with its rugged outlaw charm, was pure sensory desolation.) Jungles held secrets, surprises, complex symbiotic relationships between strange, colorful, and dangerous animals. Rich green foliage, wide stumps, spiderwebbed branches, thick, knotted roots, creeping vines, endless visceral nuance—this was the pulse-pounding aesthetic of the jungle, unparalleled by all other visual scenes except, perhaps, the spreads in *Where's Waldo* books that transposed the jungle's sprawling complexity into an urban mode—the same mode that drew me to Manhattan's "concrete jungle" years later. Jungles invited me to look, to explore intricacies on widespread pages. Even at age eleven, I enjoyed the action-comedy *The Rundown* less for its action-comedy value than for the fact that it had Dwayne "The Rock" Johnson traipsing around the Amazon.

Who would trade this lush mystery for the pre-made desolation of Flannelgraph Israel? I sometimes wonder: if the Israelites lived in Brazil or Kawaii (the magical land where I had my first, euphoric encounter with a real jungle), would I have been more attracted to Bible stories? Perhaps. But the jungle always carried an exciting, very-not-Sunday-School narrative along with it. When Elmer Elevator meets a lion in the jungle of *My Father's Dragon,* the lion yells: " 'Ordinarily I'd save you for afternoon tea, but I happen to be upset enough and hungry enough to eat you right now.' And he picked up [Elmer] in his front paws to feel how fat he was." That's a nerve-wracking image. Elmer only escapes death with a cunning diversion; by the time Daniel was lowered into the lion's den, the lions were already tranquilized by God's power. Didn't my Lord deliver Daniel? Yeah, but I kinda wished he hadn't. Why couldn't Daniel fight off the lions instead? (Ehud woulda done it!) The climax of the story of Daniel in the lion's den was no climax at all; it was an anticlimax. The jungle was always full of climaxes and Bible had almost none of them—all of its climaxes were anticlimaxes, transformed into didactic instructions about how one ought to behave, how one ought to trust in God like Daniel. They weren't dramatic stories charged with tension and narrative momentum. These were instruction manuals for how to limit one's freedoms in order to "be good" and avoid conflict.

But, oh, how this child who knew no real conflict desired conflict! He was lucky enough to have a backyard graced with an ivy-saturated back wall, lined by a long planter thick with deciduous shrubbery, and, every spring, red, pink, blue, tropically vibrant impatiens. So he would traipse, like Dwayne "The Rock" Johnson himself, though *his* Amazon: the skinny corridor between the planter and the ivy where the shrubbery was just tall enough to go over his head, where shadow and mystery reigned supreme, where anything could happen before—phew!—he escaped back into the grassy clearing once again.

Here's the part he wouldn't admit, though: as much as he loved the jungle, he needed that grassy clearing, too. Although Sunday School presented a mechanically produced, Koonsified, reduced, yada yada image of boring, ethical safety, the world of *endless* jungle was just too frightening. The mind so attracted to knotty mysteries was also vulnerable to assault by the mysteries it craved. And so I remember staring at televised horrors with some combination of fascination and pain, attracted to bright colors and spastic motion with a gnawing awareness that it'd haunt my mind.

The world of endless jungle was a world in which not all big cats could be outsmarted. One of these was the housecat from *The Adventures of Spot*, my first media-fed fear, who tormented a little yellow helpless puppy via a horror movie jolt. It looked so cute, sleeping there—then, instantly, open mouth sharp teeth wild crazy eyes blood-curdling "MEOW!!!"

The jungle of Never-neverland was the jungle of the terrifying Cap'n Hook. Not even church functioned as a sacred haven far from that guy. Quite the opposite: for weeks on end, toddler Nathan front-ended the churchgoing ritual with a ritual of his own. "No chuhch! No *chuhch!*" he'd cry and kick until Mom, mystified and agitated from fit after fit, put her hands on her hips and leaned toward the changing table. "What's wrong with church, Nathan? You like church!" Watery snot dripped from nose to lip and he stopped flailing: "No Cap'n Hook," he moaned. Mom talked to the nursery staff. They suspended their weekly screenings of *Peter Pan*.

On our home TV, the jungle of *Fraggle Rock*, made of knotty, underground tunnels, brought with it the tortuous intestinal jungle of Gorg, the "Big Guy," in which the Fraggles meet their ends if they are caught stealing radishes. The Big Guy looked a bit like Chewbacca if he gained three hundred pounds, got a nose job, and took a steamroller to the face. The Fraggles flee from him in a radish garden like Dario and Maria, trying not to be crushed and eaten alive by a media-made mass.

There was no escaping from the Big Guy just as, for the child protagonists of *Chitty Chitty Bang Bang,* there was no escape from the long-nosed, stringy-haired, top-hatted Child Catcher, the first and only cinematic villain to give me a recurrent nightmare. I stood alone, four years old, in a dark, menacing forest. I'm not sure if Edward Hopper painted forests, but, if he did, this would've been one of them. The tree trunks were thin but the canopy was thick, full, casting one wide, black shadow over the flat, endless expanse. I stood on a black dirt road that ran up and down the forest, utterly isolated. In the distance: *clip-clop, clip-clop,* accompanied by an ever-nearing whistle as a horse and buggy slowly, slowly, crept my way. Some fall leaves rustled in the wind, quietly. The quiet was intolerable, for I knew that the buggy was a mobile prison for children, that the driver was the Child Catcher, that he was coming for the suffocatingly shaded, totally isolated, absolutely unprotected *me*.

I had this dream in the low-key beach town of Cayucos. As it came back again and again, night after night, I took solace in those Central Coast flannelgraph views: the plain, tan beach sand and the grey morning fog and the watercolor blue sky, so different than the dark, green shadows that haunted my mind. That forest was no jungle I could explore with my own cunning. It was, like other media-sent fears, like the Bible stories themselves, imposed and pushed on me by external sources. And as my free will was swallowed by these media monsters, it was replaced with . . . visions of life without free will.

✶ ✶ ✶ ✶ ✶

The Sunday School Stories and the Secular Stories both pounced on my helpless consciousness like lions, determined to wrangle my willpower from me. The media-made nightmares were swift, brutal, merciless, medieval. Most Sunday School stories, on the other hand, pretended to be gentle, kindly offering up a boring, conflict-resolved life in exchange for a will placed at Christ's feet. But not only did that reward seem as dull as the Gorg-eaten fate seemed terrifying, it was clearly false: nobody was kindly asking me to do anything; the boredom these stories produced was no different than the boredom I was actually forced to experience, week after week, lesson after lesson, flannelgraph after flannelgraph. How was I supposed to surrender a free will I didn't even have? How much could these adults *ask* of me?

More than kids, certainly. And it was two kids that mobilized one strange, surprising break in my apathetic regard for contemporary Christian media: Benjamin with his pink, makeup-smeared cheeks and dark-brown eyes, piercing and sincere below a flexible brow primed for emoting confusion and curiosity; Sarah with her bright white teeth and spotless olive skin framed by loose curls falling onto natural fabrics draped over her shoulders, Jedi-style. These were the central characters in Inspirational Film's *The Story of Jesus for Children,* the short film Mom put into the VCR during Holy Week, an abridged and modified version of what, in the days before *The Passion of the Christ,* evangelical Christians simply called "The Jesus Film."

Mom left the room to work upstairs. I watched alone. I was seven. "The Jesus Film" was made in 1979. A monument to its time, it leaves the gritty artistic risk of the New Hollywood for the square, stilted staunchness of the 1980s. Jesus is white, bearded, blue-eyed and dull, prone to British archaisms like "verily I say unto you" and occasional bouts of hollow laughter. Mary Magdalene's prostitute profession is only suggested via sex hair: a perm so voluminous that one fears, when she leans down to kiss Jesus's feet, that his toes will tangle in it.

The film was not quite a spectacle like *Ben Hur* or *The Ten Commandments,* but it was filmed in Israel (a *slightly* less deserty place than the flannelgraphs suggest) and it nails the scope of the temple, the wilderness, and the marketplace by location shots alone. As I sat on our forest green couch with my toes resting on our burgundy shag carpet, I was intrigued: to a flannelgraph-fashioned mind, those moving, real-life Bible pictures were almost as intriguing as the dialogue was dull; they were *getting somewhere.* And the children's version mercifully cuts the two-hour run time in half and adds the type of fictional flourish that piqued my interest: "We don't know exactly how children found out the truth about Jesus," Benjamin says in his opening voiceover, "but it might have happened something like this."

The children are carefully cut into scenes from the original film. They host their own speculative debates in Sarah's family barn, too, with line readings as wooden as the structure itself: "I don't care what *you* say, Benjamin, *I* really think Jesus *was* sent by God!" "Just because he performs miracles? It could all be magic tricks!" Sarah is the believer—her grandmother knows Jesus's mother Mary—and Benjamin is brought up skeptical by his real whiner of a conservative Jewish daddy. Spoiler Alert: Benjamin changes his mind, post-Resurrection, and decides to follow Jesus. He lets his furrowed brow straight-line.

Then, suddenly, startlingly: the story cuts to a medium shot of Sarah on a stool, still in costume, framed by a brown vignette, *staring right at me.* Like the end of *The Great Train Robbery,* self-contained narrative gives way to direct address— what film scholar Tom Gunning has famously termed the century-old "cinema of attractions," the filmic hailing of the viewer, the imaginary reach outwards, from the celluloid, through the screen, with something wonderful to show—a gunshot aimed right at the heart. She says: "Well, what a great story. And it's true!" Benjamin, in close-up: "You saw and heard me make my choice to believe that Jesus is God's son, and ask Jesus to live in me." His marvelous brow furrows one more time. "Now it's time for you to make a choice. Would you like to ask Jesus to live in you now? Your answer could be: 'I don't understand.' Or: 'I'd like to talk to my mom and dad first.' Or: 'I'm just not ready yet.' Or your answer could be: '*Yes,* I want to ask Jesus into my life. I want to ask Jesus to live in me right now. I want Jesus to forgive me for all of my sins, all the wrong things I've thought, said, or done.' And you can tell him that you want to live with him forever."

Alone in my living room, before that altar of a grey cabinet-turned-TV-stand, on that green couch, on that shag carpet, I was struck. On one level, I knew I was giving into media manipulation: shows like *Blue's Clues* had been trying to wrangle my attention through direct address, fake *I'm fun and I'm in the room with you, kid!* presence, as long as I could remember. I knew that trick. And we Presbyterians were too slick for all that manipulative altar call razzle-dazzle. My Sunday School group saw kids decide to follow Christ at the Indian Village Summer Camp, but the call-to-faith was simple, the converted kids were from other churches. Nobody, and certainly no peer, ever asked me, straight-up, face-to-face, medium-shot distance away, to follow Christ. I felt trapped in Sunday School, sure, but Sunday School didn't try to trap me like that.

And away from Sunday School, away from my parents, away from the world, I let something go. I gave in. I said yes. I repeated after Benjamin. I wanted Jesus to live in me. I wanted Jesus forgive me of my sins.

When Mom came back downstairs I told her what happened, sort of sheepishly—I knew that I wasn't exactly *gliding*, falling for this video trick—but dutifully; I also knew I'd be praised for my commitment. It was the right thing to do. Mom was interested and positive and sincere—if not visibly overjoyed, exactly (we keep our emotions visible but down-to-earth in our family; we glide)—and later, when she told Dad about my commitment, he responded with similar "That's cool, Nato!"-type energy. I felt both sheepish and vindicated. I think part of me was relieved to get that inevitable conversion-thing out of the way and go on with my life. *Phew.*

I don't want to question the legitimacy of that moment—as if mystical moments of pure shift can be understood, much less measured—but I do know that I didn't actively understand, nor love, Jesus and his sacrifice for years after watching that video. I'm not sure if seven-year-old Nathan was turned off by the heightened, scripted nature of the film, but I do know that he was somehow pricked, not by Jesus Himself,

but by those two peers facing his way, looking at him, somehow piercing through the voltage, the cathode ray, the glass,
the distance, inviting him, and him alone, so softly, sweetly,
sincerely, to come along with them. Let go of yourself. Repeat
after us. You don't have to—we won't force you, you might not
be ready, that's okay!—but we encourage you. We invite you.
      They got me.

      The spirit of invitation was something that video had in
common with those blank sheets of drawing paper: they invited me to impose myself on them, to *become* through them.
The sheets asked nothing but my creative presence, required
nothing but my dedicated hand. On those sheets, I was neither swallowed by secular threats nor strapped down by didactic limitations. I explored the jungles of my mind with
unparalleled control, power, opportunity. I created stories and
worlds with all the agency I could muster.
      That storytelling impulse fed into other moments of per-
sonal freedom. Some of the most memorable moments played
out before every afternoon nap and every nightlight-bathed
snooze when I checked in with My Guys. The Trinity of Guys
consists of: (1) Brown Bear, with tight, curled, light brown
hair. Larger than the other Guys, Brown Bear is the oldest
and the wisest. He can be a bit of a know-it-all sometimes,
but his wisdom gives him strength, calm, and perseverance.
(2) Teddy, about half as large as Brown Bear, has shiny beady
black eyes and a slight knitted smile. The smallest, meekest,
and the most sensitive Guy, Teddy was nervous and frightened by The Guys' adventures. But I held his sensitivity close
to my heart, cherishing him like some vestige of my own unimpeded purity. (3) Pooh, goldenrod yellow, a little larger than
Teddy, the third Guy and my ostensible favorite—although I
cherished Teddy with a secret, burning affection that Pooh

will never know—has a personality appropriated from my beloved *Winnie the Pooh* cartoons. A bit vapid but never stupid and ever amiable, Pooh is the perfect medium between Brown Bear's steady maturity and Teddy's fretting naïveté. My special connection with Pooh was forged out of similarity. He is the sort of creature I wanted to be: neither mature enough to be a didactic Sunday School teacher, like Brown Bear, nor naïve enough to be frightened, paralyzed, swallowed by the difficult jungles surrounding us. Pooh is always open, good-natured, pleasantly inquisitive, ready for a sensible adventure. He loves and needs both types of friends—the mature, instructive ones and the sweet, sensitive, timid ones—but he wishes to be neither of them. Writing this now, I realize that my ambitions have hardly changed. Deep down, I still wish to be Pooh. I want to rest in that pleasant middle place between the suffocating and the suffocated.

And so my beloved babysitter Beth would put her ear to my door during my midday nap, as quietly as she could, to listen as The Guys talked and traipsed through my blanket-formed jungle (or my blanket-formed Hundred Acre Wood, if I wished to stay on brand), ready to uncover new discoveries drawn in my imagination. She'd listen as these animals bound themselves together to face the unknown—Brown Bear offering wisdom, mitigating Teddy's fear and guiding them in the right direction; Teddy offering pure, un-ironized sensitivity and childlike wonder, softening Brown Bear and reaching Pooh in the depth of his soul; Pooh acting as congenial glue between both extremes—with their particular form of Trinitarian joy, long before the Trinity meant anything to me. And she'd listen as my voice would soften, lessen, drift until I left the jungle for Child Catcherless sleep.

Psychologists think that imaginary friends give children opportunities to learn and practice theory of mind: the ability to attribute beliefs, desires, and intention to people other than themselves. A conversation with an imaginary friend is like a personal flight simulation before a trip to interpersonal outer space, like a practice workout on a conversational treadmill before a jump into real life's conversational marathon. Imaginary friends are mediums between a child's developing mind and the social world beyond its bounds.

When I think about my relationship with The Guys, my relationship with the worlds I drew and the stories I told, I think there's credit to that line of reasoning. But I also sense something lacking in that definition. It's too functionalist, structuralist, predetermined, premade . . . and the very joy of imaginative drawing, the joy of The Guys, was the joy of escape from the predetermined world. I drew with a sense of wide-eyed abandon that I never felt beyond my drawing table's white SoCal light. I animated The Guys with a sense of adoring empathy that I rarely felt for peers or adults, even years down the line. I liked my own mind more than I justifiably should have—and when I'm at my worst, and I'm at my worst more than I'd like to admit, I still do.

The drawings and The Guys did not just teach me that other people thought like I did. Rather, like my cousin Brody's iPhone, they offered an escape from the suffocating deadlock of the adult-formed world. They offered exhilarating liberation from media that pressed and crushed and siphoned my will, from the flannelgraphs—heightened, scripted, mechanically precise—to the Bad Guys—wild, brisk, unstoppable.

But this liberation came not through escaping the world, exactly, but through subsuming the world within the confines of my will. I felt a prickle of recognition when I read Mark Strand's review of the exhibition "Hopper Drawing," recently (posthumously) published in *The New York Review of Books*. Like Young Nathan, Hopper drew and drew, mostly preparatory sketches for his famous oils—but there's something peculiar about them: "The changes from sketch to sketch often seem so minor, each one no more than a dress rehearsal for the next, that one wonders how much, if any, information each contains, or if this was their purpose." So why did Hopper make so many sketches, if not as a means to a technical end? Strand's theory:

> They may have been a way of familiarizing himself with the subject of the painting, the ultimate aim of which was to own it imaginatively. . . . This absorption of the outer world into his inner world could only be accomplished through a protracted ritual of drawing and redrawing, slight adjustments here and there adding up to imaginative ownership and psychic freedom.[11]

Absorption of the outer world into his inner world . . . adding up to imaginative ownership and psychic freedom. I know what this absorption feels like! So did Fellini, for that matter. As much as media can press in and crush us, Fellini knew that in our own hands, mediums can allow for an exhilarating expression of free will. *La Dolce Vita* achieves its brilliance as an expression of Fellini's will. Many of the film's sequences—from the famous dip in the Trevi Fountain to the mind-haunting miracle sequence—restage actual media events as they were captured by real-life paparazzi. The film wasn't made to invent new stories; it was made to subsume the media-determined world under Fellini's creative prowess. And then, charged with imaginative ownership and psychic freedom, Fellini enters into the world, through his fictional cypher, Marcello, with all the modernist agency he can muster, searching for other ways to act as a free being in a media-choked world.

To modify Susan Sontag's razor-sharp quote:

Perhaps the best way of clarifying . . . the relation between art and the rest of human feeling and doing, is to invoke the notion of will. It is a useful notion because will is not just a particular posture of consciousness, energized consciousness. It is also an attitude toward the world, of a subject toward the world. . . . The overcoming or transcending of the world in [*La Dolce Vita*] is also a way of encountering the world, and of training or educating the will to be in the world.[12]

So it was with my drawings, my Guys. My overcoming or transcending of the world with my own fictional worlds was also the development or training of a will strong enough to enter into the world. It was the creating of a free self that could traverse the jungle without being crushed, like Dario and Maria, by the Sunday School teachers, by flannelgraphs, by Big Guys, by Captain Hook, by the Child Snatcher, by Facebook timelines. The Guys and the drawings were mediums between the helpless, Teddy-like child that was and the free will that was to be: the will that, years and years down the line, I'd slowly, ever-so-slowly, try to relinquish at the feet of others, at the feet of Christ—really.

But let's not get ahead of ourselves.

Haman: Ready For His Close-up, June 6, 2004

CHAPTER 2

CELEBRITY IMAGE

M<small>Y</small> <small>WILL</small> developed slowly. I was a shy kid in public, with strangers. There was probably some temporal threshold above which—after six hours with one group? Two days? One week?—I'd start to let loose, and by then I'd maybe even act like a goofball or a jackass. But I hated talking to strangers, even if they were my own age. I refused to ask for ketchup and mustard from the McDonald's counter.* I've gotten better,

---

* This is why I stare at New Yorker kids—raised with unaccountable levels of confidence and swagger as if the whole world is one giant stuff dispensary just for them—with a sense of bafflement and wonder. When a fourth-grade-ish stringy-haired boy walks up to a coffee shop counter

slowly, though practice, desensitization, cycles of risk-and-reward; I can now approach strangers without feeling choked by dread (unless those strangers happen to be celebrities I admire or females at bars). Nowadays, I can even small talk with waiters and baristas and bartenders and then feel a bit like throwing Mary Tyler Moore's beret: I'm gonna make it after all.

But as I dip further and further into adulthood, I realize that cocktail-party-type socialization will never be easy for me. Exciting, maybe. Important, certainly. Natural? Never. I still stare at hundreds of accepted grad students in a wide, lavish ballroom—intellectual people, right? Bookish people, right? Anti-social people, right?—caught in the middle of buoyant, wine-soused conversations with brand-new-BBF-looking folks and I have no idea how to enter into the fray. When I grab a slice of pie with a friend in Gowanus, I still have to pack my mental bags beforehand to make sure I'm emotionally and psychologically prepared to engage and look engaged, to ask questions and have answers for questions, to focus my attention and look like I'm focused, to learn to keep my buzzing phone in my pocket and figure out how to be present.

It's not easy, but there is something about a latte-sipping body that spurs me into determined action. Part of this is selfish: if I'm present, listening, responsive, then the person may think I'm a likeable person. But there's another sense in which a moving, blinking, smiling, crying physical mass draws me out of my solipsistic cave, alerts me to something inherently valuable. And then I have biblical scaffolding to lean on: I'm

---

that's taller than him and asks for a cortado and an almond croissant for his mom, who stands outside with one hand on her stroller and the other on an iPhone 6 held to her distracted ear, I think: *what Planet did this boy grow up on?*

told that we're all parts of one body, that the greatest lovers give up their lives for their friends, that we are to be one as God is one. So I pray more during conversations than at any other points. My prayer usually goes something like: "God, let me engage with this person, let me listen to this person, let me embrace this person, let me be honest with this person, let me love them as I love myself, let us be one." But it takes work; I don't really know what it looks like to love someone as myself; my conception of oneness is muddied at best, occluded at worst. I need help.

It's comforting that Jesus knew how hard this could be, since he felt that he had to pray a version of my prayer on my behalf: "Holy Father, protect them by the power of your name, the name you gave me, so that they may be one as we are one" (John 17:11) In fact, despite the slightly confusing use of the present tense ("as we *are* one") Christ had to ask for the same oneness, the same bilateral glorification, that he requested on our behalf: "And now, Father, glorify me in your presence with the glory I had with you before the world began."

In churchy settings, people often mention the sheer contrast that lies between the ebullient oneness Christ experienced when he and God were one, before the world began, and the suffering he felt on Earth, the suffering that culminated in the absence he experienced on the cross. It's a fine point, but, rereading this prayer, I have to wonder if one of the Man of Sorrows' many sorrows arose from the fact that, on earth, he had such a direct, intimate line of connection with the Father while he was, simultaneously, so distant from bilateral glory he knew so well, distant enough to ask for it, to weep for it. How infuriatingly difficult it must have been to be so close, so tantalizingly *near* the Father's warmth, yet so, far, far away. And I suppose this agonizing closeness-but-farness was perpetuated not only through Christ's intimate prayer life, his shared consciousness, but through the Image of God stamped onto and beaming out of the faces of those who had turned so far from God. The Image of God without the presence of God: Christ dying of thirst in the middle of the blue, wet ocean. "Jesus, knowing that all things had already been accomplished, to fulfill the Scripture, said, 'I am thirsty'" (John 19:28, NASB).

★ ★ ★ ★ ★

Image without presence: perhaps that's why I hate Skype. Or, more accurately, perhaps this is why I'm *scared* of Skype. Even when I spent a semester in Prague, I talked to my parents via Viber—an audio-phone-via-Internet app—instead of Skype.

In March, I received a Facebook message from an old friend of my parents: "I would love to meet with u . . . Can u skype? What is your email?"

"My email is nathan@nathandroberts.com. It's the easiest way to reach me. Would love to talk to you more too!"

"Skype? This is an opportunity for cross generational, cultural, film school, I can't miss this opportunity to break bread . . . even via skype!"

"nah I'd love to Skype with you in theory, but i'm not on Skype, and I do have a busy couple months ahead. That said, my family is actually moving back to LA soon, so I'll be there a lot more often and we can actually meet in person!"

I lied. I'm "on Skype," though the app is never on. But the notion of Skyping—with a borderline-stranger, no less— makes me wither. I'd rather not talk to someone at all than talk to them via Skype. Apple's Facetime program is a little bit better, but, still . . . no.

While my social anxieties are mine and mine alone, perhaps I feel an exaggerated version of a more general animosity.

(That would be comforting, wouldn't it?) If movies tell me anything, I know that Skype is used by highfalutin' executives in their big-windowed, shiny-oval-tabled penthouse conference rooms where the resolution looks stellar and the conversation never lags (both unlikely occurrences in my real-life Skype experience) and the future is now.* But I know so few people who use Skype or Facetime in their civilian existence. Let's guess that for every Skype call made worldwide, one million text messages are sent. That might be an underestimate.

Why do we collectively pass Skype by? Image without presence? Perhaps. But what is it about an image that seems so much more repulsive than an instant message, a text message, an emoji, these things that provide even less presence than pictures and videos? Shouldn't we just take what we can get—144p, 240p, 360p, 480p, 720p, 1080p, virtual reality and beyond?

In his dystopian behemoth *Infinite Jest,* David Foster Wallace not only predicts that we'll give up videoconferencing, but he explores—in his loopy, exaggerated way—why images give us anxiety. His book is set in a possible future world, so he explains, in past tense, "WHY . . . THE TUMESCENT DEMAND CURVE FOR 'VIDEOPHONY' SUDDENLY COLLAPSED LIKE A KICKED TENT . . . WHY THE ABRUPT CONSUMER RETREAT BACK TO GOOD OLD VOICE-ONLY TELEPHONING?"[13]

---

* The TV show *Veep*, ever willing to cut through glossy fantasy, is the only show I know that portrays the Skype/Facetime I know well. Amy, Selina Meyer's campaign manager, is stuck in traffic. She Facetimes into an important campaign meeting. Ben is indignant: "Oh, can't she just call in? I feel like I'm on trial in the future." Amy's shouting voice breaks up like a robot with failing batteries. Her face is stretched by the iPad's wide-angle lens. The video skips through a series of choppy still frames before freezing on her frown: wrinkles shoot up between the bridge of her nose and her slanted eyebrows; her mouth is puckered like a malformed geode. "Ah . . . okay. I can't look at that anymore," Selina says. This is the Skype I know.

Wallace traces a historical-emotional development: first, video conferencing caused emotional stress because it broke an illusion. When we talked on the phone, we didn't have to give our full attention to the person on the other end of the line—we could "look around the room, doodle, fine-groom." But because "the phone-line's other end's voice was dense, tightly compressed, and vectored right into" our ears, we imagined "that the voice's owner's attention was similarly compressed and focused"—even though we were distracted. "This bilateral illusion of unilateral attention was almost in-fantilely gratifying from an emotional standpoint: you got to believe you were receiving somebody's complete attention without having to return it." It was a classic case of Golden Rule breakage: we expected attention from others that we re-fused to give unto them.

"Video telephony rendered the fantasy insupportable. Callers now found they had to compose the same sort of earnest, slightly overintense listener's expression they had to compose for in-person exchanges." To do anything else would be rude and disrespectful. Hence the stress: *Do I look interested enough? Present enough? Likeable enough?* Even worse was "the traumatic expulsion-from-Eden feeling" that bubbled up when we realized that the person on the other end of the line didn't look as interested, present, and like-able as we'd assumed over the audio-phone. We realized that our self-centered audio-telephonic assumption was, in fact, a delusion: we "were actually commanding not one bit more attention than [we] were paying."

Vanity worsened this stress. We got more and more ob-sessed with how we looked during video calls. "This sort of appearance-check was no more resistible than a mirror," and just as horrifying. As we got more and more self-conscious, tech companies swooped in to help. Normal, everyday makeup was one-upped by High-Definition Masking. Masks were composited from a variety of pictures and "combined into a wildly attractive high-def . . . face wearing an earnest, slightly overintense expression of complete attention." But that wasn't enough cosmetic correction: "consumers . . . began preferring and then outright demanding videophone masks that were really quite a lot better-looking than themselves were in person. . . . Stronger chins, smaller eye-bags, air-brushed scars and wrinkles . . ."

Therefore, in a final twist, all of videoconferencing's advantages—borderline-unmediated, nearly-present conversation with distant people—were undercut by mask-made mediation. Covered by masks, video callers were just about as distant as they were during voice-only telephone conversations. They were "once again stresslessly invisible, unvainly madeup."

Videoconferencers slowly realized that that they were staring at illusions even more heightened, manufactured, and commodified than Dario and Maria's "miracle" in *La Dolce Vita.* They realized that they were presenting and receiving simulations of presence, nothing more, so they gave up videoconferencing all together: "a return to aural-only telephony became . . . a kind of status-symbol of anti-vanity."

Wallace's scenario is funny and strange and clever, and, more importantly, it provides an illuminating, exaggerated point of comparison for what actually happens as technology improves.

When I first instant messaged, via Apple's iChat program, I spoke to my cousin Dustin. I was a fifth grade newbie; he was in middle school, with the program. A literal shiver of excitement flooded through my body when those first multi-colored text bubbles blooped onto the right side of the white box on my iMac desktop computer. When he took pictures with his webcam, wearing a dark gray sweatshirt that blended in with that moppy black loofa of an afro he sported back then, it was even more impressive. Even though he lived in North Hollywood, an hour away, he felt so mysteriously *present*. This technology paved the way for video chatting apps like Skype. It was an advance if there ever was one.

Dustin held my rapt attention during that conversation. I only left our chat window* to Google the definition of "brb," an acronym he used (an acronym that might be dead? Remember when we once politely *told* people that we'd "be right back" instead of merely ignoring their Facebook messages and text messages until a convenient moment arrives?). *Huh, I* thought. *So it's okay to get up and leave when you message people like this. That's . . . kinda weird. Okay.* I felt a version of what Wallace called the "bilateral illusion of unilateral attention": *of course both parties must prioritize each other during conversation. Otherwise, why would they be on instant messenger at all?*

But soon enough, I began talking to friends who wouldn't "brb"; they just wouldn't respond to my messages for long periods of time while they were clearly doing other things— and clearly assuming that I was doing other things, too, since they didn't apologize for their behavior or act like there was anything abnormal or disrespectful about it. I didn't quite experience a "traumatic expulsion-from-Eden feeling," but it was annoying and a bit discomforting—until I began to diverge from IM conversations while I waited for them to get back to me. And I realized that I wasn't only free to "look around the room, doodle, fine-groom, peel tiny bits of dead

---

* Funny how we call them "windows," as if we can peer right through them to see the other person's image looking right back at us.

skin away from [my] cuticles"; I could call to my mom in the living room, use the restroom, play Superkid on Freearcade. com. (I played that a lot.) This became a regular habit, one I shared with my conversation partners. I'd sit at my iMac with multiple Internet windows open, instant messaging in the background, giving those windows half or less-than-half of my attention, assuming that the other person on the line was also giving me less-than-half of their attention, too.

Instant messaging was not only more technologically advanced than the telephone: it left the stakes even lower than the telephone. When Mom talked on the phone, she had drawn out, multi-hour conversations with ebbs and flows and points and counterpoints and confessions and responses and giddy arcs like scenes in well-crafted fiction. As she walked around the house completing various chores with the cordless wedged between her shoulder and ear, I listened to those mature, orchestral movements with a sense of awe: *so this is what it means to talk like an adult.* To talk on the phone was to be present, attentive, always ready with an active response or an interesting counterpoint. To talk on the phone was to have a fully developed, fully interested, giddily extemporaneous sense of self. And so, as my developing self marshaled the courage and will to enter the jungle, the phone was a sign of how far it had left to go: it sensed the distance between the comfortable base camp it lounged at and the interpersonal summit it knew it needed to climb, but couldn't. The phone was a little plastic source of existential despair.

If the phone line was a mountain, the iChat box was a molehill. I could climb with confidence in the tools at my disposal. It wasn't because I was a better climber—although, since I've always been a better, more concise writer than an extemporaneous speaker, plastic keys did make better crampons than my often-hesitant vocal cords. It was because the summit was so much lower. I had the instant gratification of instant messages, but, crucially, I had the freedom to enjoy them at my own pace, to respond to them whenever I wanted to. I could socialize at a near-conversational speed without the burden or sacrifice required for a full-on conversation: no need to look the other person in the eye (a requirement that still makes me uncomfortable), to indicate that he or she is the sole recipient of my thoughtful attention (he or she rarely is). Instant messaging had all of conversation's benefits with none of conversation's burdens. The ball was in my court, permanently—unless, of course, I was trying to have an intense conversation with someone who wouldn't reply to my messages.

In a recent essay, Joshua Rothman explains the trajectory of Matthew Crawford's book *The World Beyond Your Head: Becoming an Individual in an Age of Distraction*:

> Crawford argues that our increased distractibility is the result of technological changes that, in turn, have their roots in our civilization's spiritual commitments. Ever since the Enlightenment, he writes, Western societies have been obsessed with autonomy, and in the past few hundred years we have put autonomy at the center of our lives, economically, politically, and technologically; often, when we think about what it means to be happy, we think of freedom from our circumstances. Unfortunately, we've taken things too far: we're now addicted to liberation, and we regard any situation—a movie, a conversation, a one-block walk down a city street—as a kind of prison. Distraction is a way of asserting control; it's autonomy run amok. Technologies of escape, like the smartphone, tap into our habits of secession.
>
> . . . It's not just that we choose our own distractions; it's that the pleasure we get from being distracted is the pleasure of taking

action and being free. There's a glee that comes from making choices, a contentment that settles after we've asserted our autonomy. When you write an essay in Microsoft Word while watching, in another window, an episode of *American Ninja Warrior*—trust me, *you can do this*—you're declaring your independence from the drudgery of work. When you're waiting to cross the street and reach to check your e-mail, you're pushing back against the indignity of being made to wait.[14]

And when you're surfing the web while you're instant messaging, you're declaring your semi-independence from the stressful, adult world of bilateral attention and bilateral focus. It's the perfect interaction for a young self-in-the-making, a self that longs to assert the autonomy it's working so hard to achieve. Conversations don't have to be limiting like Sunday School classrooms, do they? Of course not. They can be little windows that we turn away from and return to at our leisure. We can be connected to each other and, in some fundamental way, free from each other, at the same time.

My generation knows this pseudo-connection well. In his essay on "Hipster Aesthetics," Ben Davis refers to the artist Dominic Nurre's *Objection Room* installation, which features openings for anonymous public sex in its walls. Nurre, born in 1980, stands at my generation's far end, but he still explains his work like this: "I'm attracted to the thought of something being nourishing and constructive but at the same time not allowing a real community to grow."[15] Well, there you go.

It is interesting, then, that iChat's next technological leap turned from the freedom of text messaging to the cage of video messaging. Although the same technology undergirds both instant messenger and Skype—they have what a philosopher might call the same "ontological basis"—a phenomenologist might say that Skype's *noeme*, its "perceptual content," is totally different. With Skype, perceptual data increases tenfold. And with that perceptual data, unlike with instant messenger, "there was of course no such answer-as-you-are informality." "Callers now found they had to compose the same sort of earnest, slightly overintense listener's expression they had to compose for in-person exchanges." *Do I look interested enough? Present enough? Likeable enough?*

At this point, Wallace delves into some of the thematic territory he tracks through best, territory that a girl in my *Infinite Jest* class aptly labeled the "artifice of countenance," which is closely related to what Magritte called "The Treachery of Images." When we talk about this sort of thing colloquially, we talk about the "masks we put on." And in Wallace's world, people turn from "composing . . . slightly overintense listener's expressions" to composing literal masks to purchasing images of totally doctored, totally different bodies. With every enhanced image we produce, we push ourselves further and further from how we look, how we really are, present in flesh and blood.

In some ways, this is nothing new. Western philosophers have long been concerned with images' capacity to underrepresent information. In *The Republic*, Plato wrote that an image "is far removed from the truth, for it touches only a small part of each thing." Plato scoffed at imitative art, calling it "only an image." These concerns reached fever pitch in the twentieth century as heightened, commodified, machine-made images began to proliferate. Theorists like Walter Benjamin described how, for "The Work of Art in the Age of Mechanical Reproduction," the artwork's "aura" of presence crumbled.[16] Enter Fellini. Enter the Flannelgraph Makers.

One of the most interesting personal and intellectual approaches to this question occurs in an essay by Roland

Barthes called *Camera Lucida*. For Barthes, photography is intimately—almost paradoxically—connected to both presence and absence. A photographic image allows for a real, physical connection between the viewer and the thing photographed. "In Photography," he writes, "the presence of the thing . . . is never metaphorical."[17] Light allows for a literal connection: "Light . . . is here a carnal medium."[18] Light is a *carnal* medium: it's an intimately physical thing; it's of the body; it links two separate, physical bodies through a "sort of umbilical cord."[19] These things can even provoke physical reactions; you can feel like you've been pricked as you look at them. ("This *some-thing* has triggered me, has provoked a tiny shock."[20]) In Barthes' most significant example, photography allows him to find "the truth of a face [he] had loved"—his mother's face.

But this is when the twist arrives: Barthes mother is dead. Her presence may not be metaphorical, but she's not physically *there* when he looks at the picture. This paradox is revealed in the full quote I abridged earlier: "light, *though impalpable*, is here a carnal medium" (emphasis mine). Like a ghost, Barthes' mother is somehow both carnal (physical, sensual, of the body) and impalpable (intangible, insubstantial, immaterial). Therefore, Barthes labels the image's *noeme* "*That-has-been*." His mother has been, but his mother isn't here now: "[the object in the image] has been here, and yet immediately separated; it has been absolutely, irrefutably present, and yet already deferred."[21]

Although *Camera Lucida* is a theoretical text, it is theory written from a place of mourning. Barthes is clearly trying to get a grip on the ghost-like woman he sees in the photograph, a woman who is neither fully present nor absent, who is carnal but impalpable, who he continually reconnects with through the umbilical cord of light, but who shocks him with her incontrovertible distance.

I felt like Barthes once. When I was eleven, we got a golden retriever puppy. We named her Mandy, a version of a name that means "Beloved." She was our first dog. It's difficult to describe how hard I fell for that little fluff ball. I woke up every morning that month with a soft little tongue on my face as she clamored over the hills and valleys of my bed, sniffing and chewing on my Guys. She was so mouthy and buoyant that we had to play fetch with her just to keep her from destroying our toes with her pinprick teeth.

Mom was playing fetch with pieces of kibble on the afternoon of Friday, April 30, 2004, when Mandy, eleven weeks old, choked on a piece, asphyxiated on her vomit, and fell into a coma. Dad carried her into the house. His face crumbled. She hung from his arms. Blood dripped from her puppy mouth. I hit the ground, on my knees. After a wrenching night during which she lay, limp, her oxygen machine-pumped, he woke me up. His voice cracked in the middle of the sentence: "Nathan, it's time to say goodbye to Mandy." We petted her fluff-ball hair one last time. Her air-pumped lungs made it bristle and flatten, bristle and flatten, bristle and flatten.

A couple days later, after I assumed that I was physically incapable of crying any longer, I found a video on the family camcorder that I had totally forgotten during the chaos. I'd filmed it as my sister Kara crammed for piano lesson: bits and pieces of "Morning Has Broken," over and over again. Mandy, nestled under the piano bench, chewed on a plush toy and a Nylabone. The camera pushed toward her, at her little level, in the most intimate shots we ever filmed. She looked at the camcorder, sniffed at it, sniffed at me holding it, cooing at her. She was so giddy, so *alive* as I filmed this—just ten minutes before she choked. And so, watching this footage again, with its palpable, miniDV texture, I broke down. She was so close, so intimate, so damn near present—but so far, far beyond the chasm that separates life from death. She *was*, she certainly was, but then she wasn't. It was like a cruel magician's trick, this image without presence. *The truth of a face I had loved. This has been.*

By the time Wallace wrote *Infinite Jest*, the pressing issue of what images lack had both mutated and grown in its accusatory urgency: how do images not only withhold information, but also actively lie and harm us when we make them? Wallace wrote about mass media often. But Wallace's writing is prescient and continually relevant because he knew that our biggest problems are not the images we're subjected to, the images that *passively* lack, but the dishonest images we *actively* compose, the images that we use to distance our true selves from others. *Infinite Jest*'s antagonist, as far as it has a singular antagonist, is a video which, when viewed, produces a state of ecstasy-turned-bowel-emptying-paralysis. People cut off their own digits to keep watching it; the video more or less forces viewers to believe that it is all that matters in the world. But it's not a video made by a major studio or a mega-corporation; it's a series of images created by a low-budget experimental filmmaker. And when we choose to watch, we're the ones who ruin our own lives. Images don't just tease us with mothers or dead puppies. We're the ones who actively produce and consume images that lie, every single day.

✶ ✶ ✶ ✶ ✶

Mom scrolls through pictures of high deserts and spiky green plants and stucco buildings and polychromatic blankets and a smiling pair: "They had such a fun anniversary trip to Santa Fe," she says.

Dad: "Yeah, except they were actually sick the whole time. They spent most of the trip in their hotel room. It was awful."

Mom pauses.

"Really? . . . Huh. Well I didn't see *that* on Facebook. That's . . . interesting."

I watched Mom's brain churn through the implications of that realization. But what's just as interesting, perhaps, was how unsurprised I was, how I wanted to say: "Of course! Of course your Facebook friends were lying! Of course your Facebook friends wouldn't post that they were puking their guts out throughout their anniversary trip. Of course they wanted to look happy. It's the artifice of countenance, Mom."

My mom's Facebook and my Facebook are a little different, though. In my Facebook, it's more popular to share articles written by others than confessional, self-penned paragraphs. (It didn't used to be like this. I look back though my digital time capsule, the Timehop app, and see confessional, paragraph-long status updates. It's embarrassing.) On my Facebook, photographs are subject to the scrutiny of carefully-curated Instagram filters. We Instagrammers know that we're faking it—of course it's all heightened, self-scripted, commodified. What else is new?

On my mom's Facebook, friends write multi-paragraph posts about how their children struggle with Williams' Syndrome or how they're moving and need prayers. My mom shares Sheryl Sandberg's soliloquy about mourning her husband. (Mom: "This has stayed with me all day. May be the best and most moving account about grieving I've ever read.") She starts her posts with statements like: "In light of all the mess of this world . . ." or, unabashed: "Love this!" For my therapist mom, the artifice of countenance holds little weight. Or, more accurately, her computerfied artifice rarely shakes off the norms of in-person interaction. It's not that she lacks an artifice; she's not one of those dreaded, indiscriminate oversharers. There are many things she chooses not to post. (If I'm involved, she'll often ask me: "Should I post this on Facebook or not?") But it's never different than what she'd say in a public conversation. She's an adventurous conversationalist and an adventurous Facebooker. "I like to go to that sad place," she says. She likes to go to that sad, honest place on Facebook, too.

As much as I genuinely admire her candor, it makes me uncomfortable more often than I'd like to admit. I'm sure this is partially because she's my mom—moms are supposed to make their children uncomfortable or whatever—but that's not all. I feel uncomfortable whenever *anyone* posts like this. It feels . . . maudlin, brash, uncensored. Like . . . how to describe it?

Like when a celebrity says something that she should've run by her publicist first.

The celebrity is the household example of the "inauthentic" person-turned-image and Andy Warhol is the perfect example of the unintentional Philosopher of Celebrity. Warhol was known for brilliantly peculiar quotes like: "I love Los Angeles. I love Hollywood. They're beautiful. Everybody's plastic, but I love plastic. I want to be plastic." "The most exciting thing is not doing it. If you fall in love with someone and never do it, it's much more exciting." "People sometimes say that the way things happen in the movies is unreal, but actually it's the way things happen to you in life that's unreal. The movies make emotions look so strong and real, whereas when things really do happen to you, it's like watching television—you don't feel anything." "If you want to know all about Andy Warhol, just look at the surface of my paintings and films and me, and there I am. There's nothing behind it."[22]

There's nothing behind it—just surface image, no hidden "presence" or "depth." Warhol was the champion of this sort of active negation, of whittling down undesirable complications. With Warhol, everything's simplified, hollowed out, flattened into images. Skin is hardened into solid plastic; people fall in love and don't do it; Warhol feels like he's watching television—he doesn't feel anything.

Warhol tried his best to help others simplify themselves, too. He not only made physical images in his Factory; he famously turned people into Superstars, allowing them to be defined by their surface-level gloss. He did this by taking them wherever he went—to parties, clubs, other glossy locations—and he also use the mechanism of the camera, the image's lack, to help them out. He's famous for his *Screen Tests*. He made them by sitting people in front of his Bolex and instructing them to stare at it without blinking, for three minutes straight. In the *Screen Tests,* even moving pictures were reduced into still photography and moving people are reduced to static images. Warhol often showed *Screen Tests* at parties and music venues, as if to encourage his Superstars-in-the-making: *This is what you can be! This is what you're aiming for—life as a still, glittering image, broadcast for all to see! There's nothing behind it!*

Many of Warhol's other factory-made films are almost as uneventful as the *Screen Tests* and they were produced to create a similar feedback loop between image and celebrity performance. Before people could take selfies to apprehend and adjust their faces, their postures, their expressions, their visual performances, Warhol was doing the same thing by different means. He'd film Superstars hanging out at the Factory (doing drugs or playing music or lazing around . . . mostly lazing around), quickly develop the films, and show them at the Factory. This gave the Superstars the opportunity to see themselves, the images they just were, and adjust their countenances in order to become the images they wanted to be. They could make their smiles a little wider, their presence a little more natural, more controlled (or goofier, as was the case with my favorite Warhol Superstar, Taylor Mead—a character actor as far as there ever was one in Warhol's social oeuvre, and the star of one of Warhol's sillier films, *Tarzan and Jane Regained*). Edie Sedgwick, in particular, with her tinny smoker's laugh and broad white smile, became an absolute pro when it came to the "earnest, slightly overintense listener's expression."* Sedgwick quickly became an anorexic and a heavy drug abuser, so who knows what she was actually feeling during any of this, but did it matter? Just look at her shimmering surface—look how she glitters. She was one of Warhol's favorites.

Warhol knew that celebrities were made by systematic reduction, by an active, continual elemination of interiority tied to a continual buildup of a pure, flat image. I've noticed this too. My friends Cole and Dylan were child stars. As I got to know them in college, they were still near enough to their careers to be topics of sibilant conversation among NYU students. Almost everybody had an opinion: "I hear one is nice and the other isn't so nice." "I met Cole in the park and he was really cool." "I met one and he was rude." "Dylan was always my favorite." I always felt uncomfortable listening to these conversations, and even more uncomfortable if the speaker learned that I was friends with them. She would look at me expectantly, as if I could lend some sort of authoritarian opinion to the discussion. "They're . . . nice guys," I'd typically say, shrugging my shoulders. But that answer always felt a little silly—*of course they're nice guys, why else would we be friends?*—and uncomfortably vacuous. On one hand, I'm not going to gossip about my friends. On the

---

* If you're interested, Warhol's *Outer and Inner Space* (1966) is one of the few films in which you can actually see both sides of the feedback loop at the same time, and watch this sort of Factory-made performance-adjustment in action. It's far too formally complicated to elaborate on here, but check it out.

other hand, I know that by answering so simply, I'm playing into a culture in which celebrities must be either "nice" or "mean," "generous" or "full of themselves," "cool" or "not cool." By answering so simply, by giving people a simple snapshot, I deny my friends their multifaceted humanity. Their quirks and foibles and idiosyncratic opinions and all of the things that make them multidimensional friends are flattened into celebrity caricatures. Cole has made a particular stab at avoiding celebrity denudation. He has an Instagram account called Camera_Duels where he posts pictures of people who take discreet photos of him from afar, as if to say: "You want to flatten me into an image? Well I'll flatten *you* into one!"—so the last thing I'd want to do is flatten him out in my personal life.

However, when people ask me to take pictures of them with Cole and Dylan, whenever Cole and Dylan put on the artifice of countenance and smile and look like they're happy to stop in the street and put their arms around the shoulders of complete strangers, I feel little pangs of jealousy. Even though it's embarrassing to admit, I know what Warhol was honest enough to say outright: the artifice of countenance can be *fun*; it can be a relief to reduce yourself to an image, to harden into the sort of shimmering plastic that pulls people in like a tractor beam. I know this because celebrity image was a crucial aid to my developing self. It helped do what little else could: it gave my timid self confidence to enter into the jungle with hope that I could make it through unscathed, maybe even loved. The artifice of countenance saved the day.

In his essay "A Supposedly Fun Thing I'll Never Do Again," David Foster Wallace writes:

> One of the few things I still miss from my Midwest childhood was this weird, deluded but unshakable conviction that everything around me existed all and only *For Me*. Am I the only one

who had this queer deep sense as a kid?—that everything exterior to me existed only insofar as it affected me somehow?—that all things were somehow, via some occult adult activity, specially arranged for my benefit?"

I know this feeling, but with one crucial difference: I *had* an occult adult activity that reified my *For Me* intuition, and that came out of Irvine Presbyterian Church.

IPC had around 750 members when my dad was senior pastor. That's six hundred adults who knew what I looked like, who heard anecdotes about my life in my dad's sermons. If you weren't a child star, try to imagine what it's like to be known by that many people, to run into that giant crowd every single week, to know what it's like to enter a room far larger than the *Cheers* bar in which everyone (except newcomers and occasional attenders) knows your name. If you grew up in a small town, perhaps you kinda know what I'm talking about—but even then, your whole town probably didn't gather every Sunday to listen to your father tell stories about you. But in Orange County, that red, angled, squarish coastal blob near the bottom of the bluest of blue states, some small town traditions remain. One of them: pastor's kids are treated like little local celebrities.

One of the main reasons that Harry Potter felt like a revelation to me is that Harry and I were both unintentional celebrities, largely addressed by people who appreciated and loved our fathers and mothers. I know the frustration Harry felt when he kept meeting strange adults who acted like they knew him, adults who would speak of his parent's accomplishments endlessly. Some people achieve celebrity and some people, like Harry and me, have celebrity thrust upon us.

Perhaps that influenced an ambiguous line in one of my first attempts at novel writing, at age seven: "Sometimes when

I have a joyful time and I'm trying to be famous even that can sometimes go wrong." But as that line also suggests, unlike Harry, I as started to grow, I didn't abhor my celebrity status. My born-into-celebrity status gave genuine social credence to my timid self-in-development. *You're okay to many people,* church culture said. *In fact, you're even kinda special. You are known.* In his book *The Pastor's Kid,* Barnabas Piper makes an astute distinction between being "known as" the kid with the pastor dad and being *known* in a full relational sense of that word. It's an important distinction, but when people flocked to you between First and Second Service, asking you all sorts of questions about your school and plays and soccer games, it was easy to pretend that there wasn't a difference between the two.

As I grew, I turned from answering adults with my head down, hands in the pockets of my denim shorts, to playing with the most gregarious and child-friendly adults (One of my favorite games was with Mr. Steve. It required me to ever-so-sneakily untie his shoelaces as he talked to people in between the sanctuary pews until he'd catch me and yell "You big baby!" and spin me around as I laughed and laughed), to borderline-craving those walks onto the bright Sunday patio where I felt like Robert Downey Jr. walking onto the set, cherished the *your-dad-used-you-in-this-great-sermon-illustration-today* small talk that was so often lobbed my way, bathed in the limelight. By mid-elementary school I even managed to whip up my own brand of Downey-type charm, mixing the requisite earnest, slightly overintense listener's expression with a touch of sly, cocked-eyebrow, too-cool-for-school type irony. Many of the culturally savvy Rainbow-sandal-clad congregants took this eyebrow raising in style because they were Orange County citizens, after all; they knew, better than most (except perhaps Warhol) the glittering, borderline-silly nature of plastic images and the sort of aloof, wry smiles they deserved. Deep down, I think many of them knew—and, by social osmosis, many of them taught me—that public countenance was, to a large degree, artifice. I was like a Warhol Superstar, after all: a near-parody of stardom, a celebrity without any reason or right to be a celebrity. All surface, nothing behind it. I didn't really care for these hundreds of people that I appeared to speak to so intently. I didn't really give them my full attention—but I sure liked their attention on me, sure liked feeling inordinately special, inordinately famous. I didn't have to be shy with them like I was on the phone—because it was all kind of silly, kind of playful, kind of fun, wasn't it?

It was. My razzle-dazzle celebrity sheen hit braggadocio bigtime on the sanctuary stage in fifth grade when I played Haman in the children's church choir musical *Malice in the Palace: The Story of Esther*. It was, as Haman himself said in the script, in a cute little Brechtian wink, "the role I was born to play." In the play, Haman is a pathetic, petty figure in the royal court who ends up hitting the big time as King Ahasuerus's prime minister because he masters the art of smooth, sexy brownnosing; Haman slid on the mask of the overintense listener/complimenter with impressive ease, and developed a spectacularly voracious ego. The culture-savvy script riffed on everything from Norma Desmond to Sally Field at the Oscars ("You like me, you really really like me!" Haman cried, beaming at his genuflecting admirers), and I took to the stage with the sort of slimeball shallowness I'd spent years developing and keeping in the cage of "niceness" and "politeness."

In fact, the great fun of the role, for both the audience and me, came from how it threw my own church persona in front of a funhouse mirror. It was a borderline modernist move, this meta link between Haman's slimy, bombastic, image-centric egomania and my own everyday version of the same, between

Haman's underserving celebrity status and my own. Haman had developed an artifice of countenance strong enough to push his childish will up to the highest of high places. I had done similarly. Now I was able to let that will blossom, unrepressed, unhindered, into a form of garish camp. We were both in on the joke. It was a blast.

Well—mostly. Haman wasn't just a narcissistic bad boy; he was a *bad guy*—he and Hitler both dreamed of the Holocaust; Hitler just managed to succeed—and I knew that I needed to ramp Haman up to a level where he wasn't just an impish clown, but a legitimate threat. *Malice in the Palace,* while more than just a simple flannelgraph, still produced an image of a would-be-mass-killer that was a little too simple, a little too reduced. And while the show gave me a wonderful canvas to draw on, I still felt that I needed to push its contours. So I hatched a plan. In a pivotal scene, Haman, dressed in new, purple robes and a little crown, parades throughout the city, commanding one and all to kneel as he passes by. Mordecai, Esther's cousin, refuses to bow to him. "Get on your knees," Haman says. Mordecai stands tall. "Get on your *knees,*" Haman says, louder. No response. "GET ON YOUR KNEES!" It's the closest we ever get to seeing Haman's virulence in high gear, and when I performed the scene I pushed it even further, right over the edge. Bravely, defiantly, wildly, I cried: "GET DOWN ON YOUR FRIGGIN' KNEES!"

Gasps and laughter, all at once. Our choir director's eyes widened as her mouth dropped. I wasn't sure that "friggin'" would be a controversial word for a fifth grader to ad-lib on-stage, but it was certainly a controversial word for a pastor's kid to scream into a microphone at the front of the sanctuary. After the play, while congregants complimented my performance, they did so with a touch of timidity, as if they didn't want their praise to be confused with total endorsement. On the *Malice in the Palace* DVD given to every choir student, that bit was cut out and replaced with the scene as performed at the dress rehearsal. It was the first time I had been legitimately censored. IPC refused to get on its knees before me.

I felt a tinge of defiant satisfaction, having actually done something worth censoring. But I also felt a bit hurt, a bit angry. It's not like what I did was *that* bad. And by cutting down my recorded image, the church cropped the full image I wished to broadcast. It limited the reach of my will, cut down my self-in-the-making with its moralistic timidity, with the script's own limited, ethically questionable image of a genocide-maker-as-clown.

But, truthfully, this emotional cocktail of defiance, anger, and hurt was pretty normal. Andy Warhol liked to assert that it is not only possible, but normal, to experience an activated lack—to be all image, nothing behind it. Humanists tend to read Warhol as if his tongue was permanently glued to his cheek, as if his whole life was performance art and there actually *was* something behind the droll, bowl-cut image, something we never saw. I don't know. It's certainly hard to believe in Warhol's antihumanism when people like Wallace and Barthes, on the other hand, movingly speak of a substantial desire that rests behind broadcast images. For Wallace, there's often a significant, substantive selfishness behind them, the selfishness that so beautifully sifts to the surface in *Infinite Jest*'s phone and video conversation analysis: we want to be loved without having to love; we want to look like we're really interested in other people when we're really just concerned about being liked for our attentive façade. Behind our projected images lies a deep psychic vanity, one that we never broadcast.

And behind the cool image I projected as I paraded around IPC as a little socialite prince lay a vanity that wanted to compensate, that *needed* to compensate, for all the time that it was frustrated, hindered, trapped within the walls of that very church. For even as I grew in social courage, as I educated myself in the artifice of countenance, the censor-some flannelgraph traps still refused to abate. And as I developed an inordinate sense of my free will in the restrictive Sunday School world, I would often ditch my attentive-meets-playfully-knowing celebrity image for a brasher, darker, and more desperate medium: defiant comedy.

Good Role Model at Christian Summer Camp, June, 2013

CHAPTER 3

DEFIANT COMEDY

As I WRITE, I'm ending the third season of *Veep*, nearing the fourth. I'm into it nowadays. One of the unique, fun things about quickly catching up on a TV show is that tweaks and improvements that took years to enact take form over a couple hours on your living room couch. It's a past tense, sped-up version of what we love about television in the first place: we can track malleable stories over a temporal expanse and observe how they shift as they're sustained by a "call-and-response"-type interaction between writers, characters, and audiences. Because television is one of the most collaborative storytelling mediums, the best shows often stumble forward, bolstered by group interaction, by a sort of collective will surging toward mutually felt truth.

This is particularly true of comedies. They're less dependent on writers withholding information from audiences—no "WTF is the Smoke Monster???" tension needed—than on writers sowing personalities that germinate within actors and blossom in symbiotic situations charged with comedic potential. The comedy writer is less a God-like *auteur*, a Singular Maestro, than a vessel for interpersonal growth. Livewire connections—between kooky characters, between characters and audiences—matter most.

Veep has formed nicely over time. It began as a clever, if rather one-note, sitcom that felt more like a parody of *The West Wing* than anything else. The opening credits mimic that show's patriotic, orchestral sweep with swaths of red, white, blue. (They also sum up the backstory with newspaper headlines: "Senator's White House Run," "Might it be 'President Meyer'?" and, ultimately, a dejected "Selina 'Proud' To Be Veep.") Its characters speak in revved-up Sorkinesque patter, parading their arrogance for all to see like Josh Lyman on speed.

But *The West Wing*'s screwball machismo was mostly bluster, consistently pulled aside to reveal dedicated idealists behind the fast-talking curtain. In the early *Veep*, there were no idealists behind the curtain. Not only were the show's language coarser, its insults more cutting, its jokes pitch black, but its characters seemed more like cyphers for its own Insult Maestro, showrunner Armando Iannucci, than flesh-and-blood individuals. Iannucci is a pro purveyor of lines like: "It was an accident, just like when Bigfoot got your mom pregnant." Nazi jokes pop up like weeds: "This is amazing! It's like a happy Nuremberg." "Jonah with money. God almighty, it's like if Hitler could fly!" "[Let me put on lipstick] so when it hits 2 A.M. my eyes will say Holocaust, my mouth will say Carnival." "If Hitler were alive right now he'd be very anxious to distance himself from me at this very moment."

There's some essay waiting to be written about how these characters embody snarling, no-holds-barred Internet commenters, but, regardless, they don't quite work. These people would say anything and everything, but their voices are Iannucci's, though and through. *Veep*'s early audience was pummeled by his simple, insistent cleverness. It wasn't welcomed into an interpersonal situation.

However, throughout the second and third seasons, thematic elements planted in the first season began to blossom. *Veep*'s meanness only wavered slightly, but it rooted its aggressive instincts in the culture of Washington, D.C., with greater success. Washington is not, after all, the sort of place where a Vice President can run around spitting hard F-bombs all over the place, utterly ignored by anyone and everyone including POTUS. Washington swarms with meddling media ready to pounce at every possible scandal even more aggressively than Marcello in *La Dolce Vita*. (*Veep* gets its own threatening Paparazzo: a photographer who reads lips.) Washington is a moralistic hotbed, a Sunday School from Hell—not only ready to damn misspeakers at a moment's notice, but actively forcing as many feet into as many mouths as it can muster. For politicians and staffers alike, the only way to avoid constant penance is to adopt a form of baby-kissing, sound-bite-dropping, flannelgraphed blandness. As Selina shakes hands and points, she cries: "It's you! Look at you, there! I'm looking at you!" beaming with manic intensity.

The more *Veep* homes in on Washington's suffocating, threatening moralism, the less the profane jabs feel like exercises in calculated meanness and the more they feel like natural releases of built-up pressure, like vibrating pipes regularly ventilated. Every action has an equal and opposite reaction; an environment of pressure-cooked "niceness" will cause insensitive releases. The more we get to know the D.C. Pressure System, the more we get to know the interpersonal chemistry bubbling around inside it and the more its characters ripen.

Veep's releases are most satisfying when they occur in defiant breaches of social etiquette, like when Selina, eyes electric, mouths "f**k off" at the lip-reading photographer. Or when she approaches the sexually assaultive husband of the Finnish Prime Minister on her way out of the Helsinki airport and smiles like the Big Bad Wolf: "Where I come from, we kill people for looking at us funny. We waterboard folks who haven't even done anything. . . . So I'm coming for ya." *We kill people for looking at us funny*—Selina is finally able to use American oversensitivity, the sensitivity that leaves her publicly waterboarded day after day, to her own advantage.

A strange thing happens when I watch *Veep*, though. My roommate and I recently argued about whether Selina is a likable character. Of course she isn't likable, he thinks; she's an insufferable narcissist like all Julia Louis-Dreyfus characters. I can't argue about the narcissist part, but, weirdly enough, I hardly mind. The more that show portrays Washington as a giant puritanical booby trap, the more I feel for Selina Meyer's weariness. The more I admire her defiant grit, her profane prowess. I gel with her desire to conquer the very political ecosystem that wishes to crush her, to beat the system from inside the system. And most of all, I empathize with the two-pronged will that rests at her character's core: a longing to be politically transgressive and publicly admired at the exact same time.

I don't care that she's an egomaniac. I empathize too well.

★ ★ ★ ★ ★

I laughed when Mrs. Taylor sang to my first-grade Sunday School class. This is the first Sunday School transgression I remember. It was strange, funny, embarrassing to hear a friend's mom sing a hymn in a warbling alto voice in front of a bunch of first graders sitting on a musty blue carpet in that high ceilinged classroom. I don't remember what she sang or why she sang it, but I remember that classroom. It was my favorite classroom because the high ceiling also let in lots of natural light through its floor-to-ceiling windows. It made me feel less isolated, less trapped than the rest of the Jenny Hart Building's stark, fluorescently lit cells with their tightly closed blinds. I could look at the adjacent parking lot and the neighboring tennis courts like a prisoner in a luxury lockup. Those glass, sun-warmed surfaces promised the free future that would arrive after the seemingly endless one-hour lesson. (Do you remember how long an hour seemed back then? The dreaded length of the sixty-minute block?)

But that room did little to mitigate the impact ("impact" is a lame noun, I know; I first wrote "trauma," but that felt like too strong a term; the proper verbiage eludes me) of the experience. I laughed when Mrs. Taylor sang. Perhaps I whispered something to my best friend Aaron, the associate pastor's kid, too, before she stopped and stared at me. The few other boys who followed my lead stopped laughing. Mrs. Taylor possessed an infuriating combination of sweet, loving sincerity—which made her impossible to actively dislike—world-weary cynicism, and strong authority. She was infamous for the punishment she held over our heads: the looming threat of a special tube of bright red lipstick pulled from her purse, applied to her lips like Shoshanna in *Inglorious Basterds*, and publicly lowered onto the offender's cheek in a big, pucker-mouthed, physically, socially, psychologically devastating kiss.* When Mrs. Taylor stopped to stare at me, I felt a twinge of horror. Was The Dreaded Kiss coming my way?! Had my doom arrived?

"Nathan, it's rude to laugh when somebody sings," she said, equally threatening and measured. "Would you like to sing for the class?"

"I, uh."

"Nathan, would you like to stand up and sing for the class?"

Everyone stared. I felt a flash of embarrassment followed by a kick of adrenaline and a flush of anger. She singled me out for a public waterboarding like Selina Meyer's dreaded press, cornering me into either public submission or public embarrassment before her towering authority. But I wouldn't let her win. I couldn't slink even further into the prison cell I was already locked in. And, unluckily for her, I had just begun to feel out my surprisingly-not-bad boy soprano in Children's Choir. I had the weapon I needed.

"Sure. I'd love to."

I stood and rounded my vowels, just as I was taught. My voice quaked a bit from the adrenaline and the frustration and the determination, but I tried to sing as purely and beautifully and faux-sincerely—no, wannabe-sincerely—as I could:

---

*The threat of the kiss was for show, mostly, made for an exaggerated mental image. Only one of my classmates actually received the dreaded kiss, one of the redheaded Morton twins, either Katie or Kelsie, and once the dreaded lips touched her freckled cheek she immediately burst into tears. Mrs. Taylor quickly comforted her in the hall outside the classroom. I grew up near the tail end of the Southern California's Age of Allowable Physical Punishment. The only other teacher to threaten physical embarrassment—Mr. Kushner, who forced offenders to stand with their noses stuck to a Jack Davis Room wall for a full sixty seconds—quit teaching soon after I entered his fourth-grade class. (I feel like Foucault would have something to say about this shift, but let's not go there.)

"Praise God from whom all blessings flooow. Praise him all creatures here belooow. Praise him above, ye heavenly hosts. Praise Father, Son, and Holy Ghost. Aaaaameeeeen."

I sat back down on the musty blue carpet, resolute. I don't remember if I received applause. I very well could have. I do remember an audible wave of shock and raised eyebrows. Mrs. Taylor stared at me, silent. Who knew that the Church Goof could be so *sincere*, so *religious*, so *pure*? Her voice was still level, if a bit taken aback.

"That was really beautiful singing, Nathan," she said.

"Thank you."

She continued with her lesson. I won.

Most of my many jokes, and the trouble they caused, did not result in such a traumatic rush of shame, adrenaline, anger, and sincerity, but the basic emotional overtone of this event—the desire to win, to beat, and thereby escape, the system that impressed its moralism on me—became a common denominator. I was never attracted to badness for the sake of badness. Simple "badness" refuses to sing the Doxology in a boy soprano. I was drawn, as if by some strange, alien force, to impose my will on a system designed to crush it into homogenized, flannelgraphed "goodness." And the ultimate goal, of course, was to overcome the system in order be liked by my peers, to lead a populist revolution of dissenting attitude against the Powers That Were. You expect me not to laugh at your strange, awkward song, for the sake of "politeness"? I'll laugh, rudeness be damned. You expect me to cower in the face of public embarrassment? I'll use my pure voice to destroy your expectations. I may be trapped in your luxury prison, but I won't be your prisoner.

For those of you who were not merely trapped in prisons but legitimately mistreated in them, I can imagine that my frustrations seem rather banal or even petty. There was no legitimate child abuse in my church experience and hardly more than a variety of well-meaning, time-giving volunteers. But it was the well-meaningness, the banality, that was so frustrating. Those teachers taught and gave and handed out coloring pages and pamphlets until my pathetic brain turned to self-centered mush. I felt a bit like Steve Martin with John Candy in *Planes, Trains, and Automobiles*. If anything, my Sunday School experience is a testament to the fact that we (and by "we," I mean "I") can push back against any power exerted over us for a long enough period, no matter how genial. Revolution brews in our blood. It also points to a crucial imaginative lack on my part: for such a creative kid, I lacked the will to even try to imagine what it'd be like to deal with kids like me as an authority figure, much less why an adult would even *want* to be an authority figure.*

So I ran when they told me not to run, spat when they told me not to spit, talked, joked, disrupted. I played a game with Aaron in which we tried to slide and launch old, hardcover Bibles from one wobbly foldout table to the next. Most of them flopped on the carpet, lamely. I'd spring a gag-ditty on less intimidating teachers, dancing around the whole expanse of the classroom, mid-lesson, shouting on pitch: "I'm Uncle Sam. Welcome to my show. I love my show, I love to hug and kiss it. For I. Am. Un-clle SAAAAAMMMMM!!" (Why Uncle Sam? What was his show? Did I want to insult America and the church at the same time? Poke at two birds

---

*The only exception to this, as far as I can remember, occurred when Janet, a lanky, extraordinarily kind woman with long brown hair and a mental impairment caused by a severe high school automobile accident, helped substitute teach one of my classes. She typically supervised babies and toddlers in daycare. As she put her hand on my shoulder and pleaded me to behave, over and over again, I felt pity, but not enough to overcome my defiance.

with one shout-sung stone? Maybe. I had no idea then. I don't know now. But the teachers were stopped in their tracks and my peers laughed and liked me and I won.)

While I loved jungles, I also loved caves. So I began to desperately search for all of the caves I could find. I planned expeditions into all sorts of the forbidding places. I hauled myself from wooden ladders into worn attics that smelled like sodden, rotting lumber. I found a hatch that led onto the roof where I'd hide in a little city of giant metal cooling-system skyscrapers. I crawled around dark, unlocked open closets. I hid in one of those closets during Worship Time, which was my least favorite part of Sunday School, perhaps because I could sense, deep down in my gut, the faux-sincerity—wannabe sincerity?—that filled that acoustic guitar-ridden space. Mrs. Taylor found me in that closet, rolled her eyes at the predictability of the discovery, and walked me back to class.

Once, during First Service, my friend Aaron and I snuck down into the basement below the sanctuary in order to steal some leftover orange juice from a refrigerator. (A beautiful thing about church kitchens: near-empty juice cartons and stale cookie trays are as omnipresent as God himself.) On our way down, as we snuck like professional spies, we took an invigorating, miscalculated risk and passed by the sanctuary's bright, gauzy back windows. The glass wasn't quite stained enough. After the service, when my dad shook hands with leaving congregants, several reported the little boys they saw sneaking out the back during the middle of his sermon.

My father brought it up to me afterward, of course. Although he and Mom were always sensitive, measured, kind when they brought up the Sunday School problems, I felt embarrassed every single time. I sat quietly in the back seat of our green minivan, looking down at the tan floor mats, trying to say as little as possible. I had such love and respect for my parents; it seemed unfair that my transgressions were brought to their attention. (Of all possible ways to curb my misbehavior, the clever Sunday School Teacher's "I will talk to your parents" threat worked best.) Not only was it embarrassing to talk about petty conflicts with these wellsprings of all that was good in my life, but it must have felt a bit like when stubborn protesters were lectured by their parents in the '60s: the conversation rested at an uncomfortable nexus between two properly separated worlds. When teachers reported wrongs to my parents they turned broad, social disputes into family issues and the problem wasn't a family problem or even—as the teachers undoubtedly assumed—a personal problem. The problem was *The System*, man! It's stompin' on my groove!

And my parents, firm and gentle, understood. Although I didn't know it at the time, Mom often stepped up to the plate as my advocate. "Do you realize how much time he has to spend in Sunday School, stuck in this building?" she'd say to teachers as she'd pull, almost demand, empathy out of them. At home, as if to balance out the moralistic suffocation, she tried to foster an atmosphere built on unimpeded honesty.

"My mom says that if I ever have a wet dream I can tell her and she'll help me do the wash," I told Mr. Gleeson, my fifth grade small group leader.

He snorted. "Yeahhh . . . you're not going to do that. Come *on*."

He was right, of course—although I was hardly quiet about that weird thing called sex that was so new and so strange. In fact, once I learned about sex, my transgressive toolkit nearly burst with brand new possibilities for shock-value humor. It was a beautiful situation: sex made a lot of people uncomfortable but it rolled off me like a bizzaro abstraction. I could poke at authorities, make my peers laugh, and come out unscathed.

I told everyone that my favorite verse was Deuteronomy 27:21. ("Cursed is anyone who has sexual relations with any animal. Then all the people shall say, 'Amen!'" It's a good thing I didn't know about Ezekiel 23:20.) I read The Song of Solomon when I felt bored; I held impromptu Bible studies to talk about it; I almost never memorized Bible verses, but I memorized that great book's first line: "Kiss me with kisses of the mouth, for your love is sweeter than wine"; my favorite sexy verse was "I am a wall, and my breasts are like towers." I shimmied around with another simple ditty: "Do you know/how to lap dance, do you know/how to lap dance?" (I had no idea what a lap dance was, but the song got *reactions*, baby.) At Indian Village I danced around the guys' side of camp in my blue and white undies. The Naked Indian dance, they called it. I took photos of Nathan Stevens' flashbulb-white butt, too. Costco refused to print them, for some strange reason.

By the time SHINE, the church-run sex-ed course for fifth graders, came around, I had to up the ante. Now that adults were talking about this sex stuff openly, without shame, my regular tricks lost their firepower. On the first night of the program I tried a new approach. I asked a doctor what the side effects of Viagra were. He looked off into the church parking lot and scratched his head: "You . . . don't need to know about that." Blackballed. *Hmmm. . . .* Finally, near the end of the course, Ms. Oehlman, the main teacher, brought out an Anonymous Questions box and I found my way in. I deposited my question: "What happens when you have sex with a cow?" She addressed the question with politically savvy evasion-disguised-as-directness, but of course I didn't actually care for her answer: I just needed Deuteronomy 27:21-style cow sex plastered in the minds of my peers and their poor parents. I won.

By the time middle school rolled around, I needed even newer tactics. In a well-worn move, I created goofy hand motions to "serious worship songs" with a couple friends, but after I was lectured by the hip young worship leader and after my mom approached him—"Do you realize how much time he has to spend at church?"—he, with my mom's prodding, decided to take me shopping for hip, young-person clothes. (Apparently my black fedora and my white-socks-with-Keen-sandals combo wasn't cutting it.) Suddenly, shockingly, an authority figure didn't want to lecture me—he wanted to *know* me, to get through my defiant jackass shield. Blackballed.

In middle school, sexual interest was treated with young-adult-professional-level seriousness by my youth pastor, Ryan, and his wife, Christi. She answered my sex-with-a-cow joke-question point-blank: "You get syphilis." I started to feel better, more respected, and I started to calm down a bit. But I was *still* stuck in that building for hours on end, and, even more significantly, a spirit of rebellion was entrenched deep within my very being. So I became a giddy, spastic improviser, eager to use all of the tools at hand for my jokes: everything from whiteout—which I'd grab from the copy room and very publicly sniff with all the nasal muscular strength I could muster, my eyeballs flying back into their sockets theatrically, my mouth opening in an expression of faux-ecstasy—to my brand-new flabby, man-boobed, love-handled body, which I'd proudly bare before the world when I'd rip off my shirt and run around the youth lounge, interrupting any and all lessons with my manic filibuster. I had no Uncle Sam song to share this time—just pure, stupid anarchy. With this shirtless gimmick, I got to poke two birds with one stone, defying Sunday School convention and conventional pubescent anxiety all at once. My personal flaw became my transgressive, two-edged weapon. I won.

Well, I mostly won. When dad learned about this shirt-less, disrespectful habit of mine, he—in a kind of surprising, newfound you-must-take-responsibility-like-a-young-adult move—asked me to send Ryan an apology email.

I did. It read:

Dear Ryan,

My dad asked me to write a letter of apology to you, for being disrespectful during Youth Group and taking off my shirt. And so now I am writing this letter. However, to be honest, I am only writing this letter because he asked me to write it. I do not feel sorry, so I refuse to claim that I am sorry. I am merely doing what he said, out of respect for him and out of respect for you. I hope to be honest in all things, in all ways, at all times. I hope you understand.

Sincerely, Nathan

With this email, as with all of my jackassadry, I tried to beat the limiting system through the system itself. I tried to be transgressive, uncooperative, and, hopefully, liked for my transgression. My peers liked my rebellion and I was even liked for that email; Ryan was impressed by my unwavering honesty, just as Mrs. Taylor was impressed by my unwavering dedication to my beautiful Doxology. But what Ryan didn't know, what I didn't even have the vocabulary to express, was *why* I wasn't sorry. How could I explain, or even understand, that my defiant will was formed by a recurring cycle of suffocating boredom and banal limitation, insensitive release, sensitive embarrassment, then adrenaline, anger, and sincerity? My desire to be funny was anything but funny—it was the crutch supporting my very sense of emerging selfhood. I felt, deep in my bones, Sir Thomas More's conviction from *A Man For All Seasons* in an inverted context: "When a man takes an oath, he's holding his own self in his own hands like water, and if he opens his fingers then, he needn't hope to find himself again."

I fell into this anti-establishment groove so entirely that when, in Middle School, the Sunday School Director gave my mom a peculiar request, I didn't know what to do: there was a third-grade boy acting out in regularly in his Sunday School class and she wanted me to help out with the class and hang out with him and help him behave. I helped, reluctantly, but like a mediocre student in Zimbardo's Stanford Prison Experiment, I quickly turned into a half-assed watchdog. After a couple weeks with zero behavior improvements in sight, I couldn't take it. My mom told the Sunday School Director, who understood but was disappointed. She thought the influence of an older friend, a role model, would inspire him to do better. I was glad to be done, but, in the back of my mind, I felt a little unsettled: *an older friend? A role model? An inspirational figure? I could* be *that?* I thought I was just called in to do the disciplinary dirty work. *What else are Sunday School teachers supposed to do?* The thought that a leader could inspire improvement by investing in him personally, by just being a self-giving with-him-because-he's-neat sort of person, never crossed my mind. I felt some newfangled aperture briefly open, ever so slightly, before quickly closing.

At age fourteen, when my family moved from Irvine to Texas, I was a clerical prisoner no longer. But years later, I realized that my desire to transgress, and to be publicly liked for doing so, still lay near the bedrock of my defiant, wounded will.

✶ ✶ ✶ ✶ ✶

It was a risky plan, but it seemed like it was working out. I was the Head Programmer at a Christian youth camp that sat at the bottom of a limestone canyon in the Texas Hill Country whittled by the tortoise-green Frio River. Programmers coordinate and implement schedules for four two-week camp sessions and every session schedule must (A) be totally unique, and (B) revolve around a plot-driven theme advanced through nightly skits. It was both an intoxicating job and a debilitating job for a creative writer with strangely unreasonable sleep needs. (I got to write a new comedic script every day, but I typically need nine to ten hours of sleep to function at my highest potential; I got around five per night that summer.) But it was particularly challenging for one central reason: I had to conform to the weirdly inconsistent censorship norms enforced by Texas Hill Country child-rearing culture while appealing to sixth graders, the youngest kids, and tenth graders, the oldest.*

This isn't to say that my go-to ideas weren't inane and insensitive by decent PC standards. I found myself, all summer long, arguing with my Co-Programmer Henry who became a skinny, swoopy-haired incarnation of the superego I never really developed. Whenever, exhausted and scrounging for material, my off-the-cusp creative ideas went too far—and, to be honest, they almost always did—he yanked me back. The original North Korea sketch had a line about cat eating in it before it was wisely scrapped. The line "Is there a pirate in there? I hope he doesn't shiver my timbers," was debated, but ultimately too funny—with its innuendo too buried—to lose. We had a long tête-a-tête about whether Harry Potter could offer Abraham Lincoln historically-themed Bertie Bott's Every Flavour Beans and say: "You better watch out for the Trail of Tears flavor, though. They're pretty salty!" before we settled on an alternative: "You better watch out for the Great Depression themed ones, though. They taste like

---

* While there were no qualms about, say, pretending to shoot Abraham Lincoln with actual shotgun blanks, anything remotely political or sexual or drug-related was totally uncouth.

burlap and sadness." (That line got a groan nevertheless.) By the end of the summer, as our energy levels plummeted along with our prudence, standards loosened: a man walks in to find his Jenga partner playing Jenga with another man and says: "Now you're cuddling up with Hernaldo like I don't even exist! Don't you remember that time we went to Seaworld and got splashed in the splash zone and got so wet?"; a Maury-type show featured a puppy paternity test; Gabe the Gluten-Free Goose needed help because Gordon the Gluten Monster was "tempting him with yeasty delights"; the king pig was called the Pork King; Viper—Swiper the Fox's badass older brother—was "meat slapped" in the face with actual pieces of sliced ham.

Somehow, all of these went off without a hitch. My risky plan, though, was for Omega Lambda Delta: a fraternity of old hippies we imagined long before the particular session in which they appeared. As Henry and I developed our nightly skit, no comedic angle came to mind. Burned-out hippies aren't spry or energetic or goofy, all of the typical summer camp sweet spots. Then it hit me: what if, in Alternate Universe Christian Summer Camp Land, instead of smoking weed, hippies breathed helium? Our old hippies, instead of using oxygen tanks, could use helium tanks. Helium is still bad for your mind so it would implicitly explain why old hippies are stupid, and, best of all, counselors could speak in helium voices—an innocent comedic slam-dunk. Henry was willing to give it a try.

Still, the drug association was risky. Step one of our plan involved approaching Ang, our boss and camp director, to explain the idea and see if the explanation alone raised any red flags. Ang, plucky, energetic, good-natured, extremely supportive, if a bit mentally scattered—as we all were at camp—thought it sounded fine. The only problem was that we didn't have any small helium tanks and we couldn't snag some in a day's time: we were left with just one gargantuan, industrial-sized missile-looking thing from the supply closet. A solution was proposed: each hippie would get his own personal balloon, imbibe its helium, and continue with the skit. Fair enough.

Henry and I wrote a script and snagged the stoneriest counselors at camp. Ganja was already on their minds to begin with. Their characters were Danny, Frank, and The Dude. The Dude's first line, spoken from a beach chair: "Well, Space Explorers, my name's Lebowski, but you can call me The Dude. . . . Before we get any further, I'm running out of air, boys. The Dude needs his oxygen." They all take hits of helium, the script commands. Henry's character points out that they're *not* breathing in oxygen. "What are you sayin,' little Bro Montanas?" The Dude asks. "We've been living off this stuff since '68." Frank adds: "It's been clearing my head for decades. I can't think straight without it. Plus my pet dinosaur shows up. Lookin' good, Tony!" They all laugh stoner laughs, the script insists. You get the idea.

From the moment they walked into the circular amphitheater, kids loved The Dude in his rainbow wig and lei; Frank in his loose lime-green sweatpants, flower print button-up, bright red vest, sweatband falling onto aviator glasses; Danny in his dangly oversized stoner poncho. There was one logistical problem, though: the Omega Lambda Delta guys were to bite or poke pinprick holes in their tied balloons. This proved more difficult than expected. The eventual holes were so small that they had trouble sucking helium out. Therefore, rather than suck out all the helium in one go and keep the show rollin' like a fresh joint, they ended up taking hit after hit, fully-baking their act. This slowed their already snail-paced rhythm. Danny legitimately forgot his lines and, embarrassed, started laughing a legitimate stoner laugh.

But our main wish was coming true: kids were laughing at the funny voices and, as I thought at the time and still think, the funny voices alone. There were a couple chuckles from one or two older guys when The Dude mentioned "living off the stuff since '68," but, otherwise, the unsoiled, camp-made minds expected camp-appropriate material and that's what they got: silly voices. So Henry and I kept the skit running along. Even when Ang popped up stage-right in our peripheral vision, waving her hands and slicing her neck with her swinging fingertips, over and over, we thought it was because she thought the skit was too long. Before Ang ran down, the sound technician talked to her about cutting our mics and cuing us off with transitional music—the modern equivalent of the ol' vaudeville hook, I guess—but we didn't know that while we performed. After the skit ended we walked off feeling so very proud, high on our own creative supply and high on the laughter of children.

Needless to say, things didn't stay happy for long. My conversation with Ang was the tensest one we've ever had. (Which isn't saying much, admittedly, since we get along with ease.) She wasn't mad. Even worse: she was disappointed. In her version of reality, the children were laughing because they all knew that their counselors were taking bong hits onstage, over and over again. Henry and I should've known better. We should've sensed the problem and cut the skit off ourselves. I disagreed and held my ground: the kids were clearly laughing at the funny voices, not the drug material.

After we talked my heart sank into that deep, sick place it went when I got in trouble. It pounded and churned for the rest of the night. My hands were clammy. I felt so defensive and upset that I hardly slept even though I was already sleep deprived. Even the next day, as we had a more level-headed, reconciliatory conversation, I reiterated my point of view and admitted my mistake half-heartedly. What I did was funny and clever and not in bad taste and I *knew* it. The skit was funny, dammit. My funny feelers didn't deceive me. Growing minds weren't soiled. I did nothing wrong. Ang just needed to smoke a bowl and relax.

Talk about honest petulance—and futility, while you're at it. I heard a group laugh at funny voices; she heard a group laugh at inappropriate material. As Mary Karr has written, "Most of us don't read the landscape so much as we beam it from our eyeballs."[23] Group laughter—that mysterious, spontaneous by-product of unexpected neurological fireworks, splayed across a web of invisible interpersonal linkages—cannot be reasoned. Comedy is a volatile, spontaneous medium.

But I think there's a deeper problem that churns at the heart of this story: why do the hippie-drug thing at all if I didn't want campers to get it? Why do any of the innuendos and the jokes that were clearly not intended for them? Children's fiction has a long history of working in two registers, of course—whether allegorical, á la *The Chronicles of Narnia*, or merely so adults won't be bored when they take their kids to the movies. But while, on some level, I was probably writing to impress attractive female counselors, I wasn't totally writing for adults, either, since I constantly feared that the actual adult camp leaders would call me out for my inappropriate jokes. I secretly celebrated every time an innuendo made it past their censors.

No, I was writing for myself.

I was supposed to be part of a team spreading the Gospel, putting kids first and putting myself last. But I was thinking of what caused an exformative release within me. As David Foster Wallace explains:

> Jokes depend on what communication-theorists sometimes call "exformation," which is a certain quantity of vital information

removed from but *evoked by* a communication in such a way as
to cause a kind of explosion of associative connections within the
recipient. This is probably why the effect of . . . jokes often feels
sudden and percussive, like the venting of a long-stuck valve.[24]

A young comic writer is utterly isolated and untested. An
early comic performance cannot display some sort of tightly
honed, audience-catered material—especially when the audience features such a diverse age range and so many possible
levels of recognition. I, out of intuition and desperation, tried
to write material that caused an exformative release in me and
me alone.

What was the bit of vital information removed from those
jokes? I realize now that it had almost nothing to do with the
comedic content of the bits themselves. It wasn't just that the
phrase "shiver me timbers" sounds sexual and sexual stuff is
funny. The vital piece of missing information was the bit of
Sunday School stuck inside me like a piece of Freudian shrap-
nel: a deep desire to please people, to get them to like me, to
love me, and to get them on my side by pushing against the
puritanical lines of taste and decency for which I still harbor
some sort of deep, abiding aversion. By designing the program for a Christian Summer Camp I was in charge of the
Sunday School World in which *I could finally call the shots*. I
could break down the System from inside the System. And my
ultimate dream was to be praised for it—that's why I slaved so
hard over those scripts, day in and day out—replacing judgment with love and substituting moralistic limitation with
gracious expanse.

But when Ang and I argued, I hit the same damn moralistic limit, once again. Different guise, same System. I was
doomed to fail, only, this time, even worse than before, I quar-
reled with an authority that I greatly respected.

Perhaps nobody, certainly nobody I've read, has captured the spirit of an immature, insufficient comedian like myself—and, by extension, the spirit of defiant comedy as a medium—better than Søren Kierkegaard. In *The Sickness Unto Death,* Kierkegaard describes the defiant will in a way that knocked me flat.

Defiance, according to Kierkegaard, happens when the will "wants to be master of itself or to create itself, to make his self into the self he wants he wants to be."[25] But the will encounters some sort of limitation, some blockage to self-formation—a parent or a personal flaw or a Sunday School prison, let's say—and feels "pained in some distress or other that does not allow itself to be taken away from or separated from its concrete self." Since it can't separate its developing self from this concrete limitation, the will internalizes the limitation. It fashions a self *by virtue of* the limitation it abhors. "[The self] wills to be himself with it, takes it along, almost flouting his agony. . . . Rather than to seek help, he prefers, if necessary, to be himself with all the agonies of hell . . ." And the defiant self, cleaving to the agony it hates, "for spite wants to force itself upon [the source of its agony], to obtrude defiantly upon it, wants to adhere to it out of malice—and, of course, a spiteful denunciation must above all take care to adhere to what it denounces."[26] Like Selina Meyer, the self wants to beat the source of its agony by cleaving to the source of its agony. Like a victim of any abusive relationship, the self cannot leave the source of its agony, because the self was formed *out of* hatred. To lose the hatred would be to lose the self, to receive "consolation [which] would be his undoing." To receive consolation, the self would have to open its fingers and let the water run out.

That was me: the child who longed to form a self by exploring the jungles but forced into the prison of flannelgraph blandness. Unable to break its chains, it internalized its limitations; it cleaved to the System and formed itself by rebelling against the System, by obtruding defiantly upon it, adhering to it out of malice. To apologize to Ryan, to admit its wrongdoing, to receive any form of grace from the system itself would be to let the self formed out of opposition run out of its fingers. And years later, to admit that my stoner comedy skit was distasteful—and not even funny due to its stoner elements—would be to let the same defiant, comedic self run out of my fingers like soiled water.

To lose a self entirely, to face a void in the place of what once was, or to cleave to a self made of malice? Even decent comedians face this problem. Mark Maron has made a career out of publicly wrestling with his internal demons; his famous podcast is called *WTF*, a cry into an existential dark if there ever were one. He addressed this problem near the end of a recent interview with Terry Gross: "Through the podcast I grew comfortable with myself. . . . I found some self-esteem that I never had, in a very genuine way, and now I just have to stop the personal growth there before I, you know, f**k myself out of the job."[27] That's a joke, but it's also a significant problem: if you've made an entire career, fashioned an entire self out of distress, to lose the distress is to lose the whole career, the whole self. As Christian Wiman, who, too, has wrestled with this problem, trenchantly warns in his brilliant, lucid memoir *My Bright Abyss*: "Be careful. . . . There is nothing more difficult to outgrow than anxieties that have become useful to us. . . . You feel at home in the world only by never feeling at home in the world."[28]

Wiman points to Giacometti, Beckett, Camus, and Kafka as exemplars of this dilemma, but even modern Christian authors can make their whole careers—or their biggest splashes, at the very least—out of criticizing the very Christian culture they cling to. Even though Donald Miller's thoughts, experiences, and writing have deepened along with his faith—*A Million Miles in a Thousand Years* is an especially inspiring, humble exhortation to, as Wiman puts it in his own memoir, "get off your mystified ass and *do* something"[29]—none of Miller's books have received as much buzz as his more explicitly critical "nonreligious thoughts on Christian spirituality" in *Blue Like Jazz.*

The popular spoken word artist Jefferson Bethke has posted several theologically inclined spoken-word poems on YouTube. As I write, "How Do You Know Someone is 'The One'?" has 1,019,405 views. "Counterfeit Gods" has 1,249,634 views. "Are Tattoos Sinful?" has 1,217,090. But what video has 29,659,910 views? "Why I Hate Religion, But Love Jesus." "Hate," that critical flare shot into cyberspace, had us all flocking.

Need I even mention Rob Bell, the controversial pastor whose *Love Wins,* a manifesto calibrated to proclaim a defiant amendment to traditional evangelical notions of Hell, shot him onto the cover of TIME magazine? Or *Relevant* magazine with its clickbait article titles like "No, Not Everything Happens for a Reason," "What We Get Wrong About Women Submitting to Their Husbands," "Being A Christian Doesn't Look Like You Think It Should," "7 Truths About Marriage You Won't Hear In Church," "4 Lies The Church Taught Me About Sex"?

In all of these cases, the Kierkegaardian pattern seems to churn beneath the surface. An impediment to religious self-formation—"religion," Hell, platitudes, wife submission, sexual mores, and so on—is acknowledged. But instead of forming a self by privately questioning and even distancing himself from what seems restrictive or untrue, the writer develops a critical persona, a writerly self, in opposition to these mores, a self that exists *by virtue of* the limitations and problems it takes issue with. The writer forces himself upon his source of agony, defiantly obtruding upon the Evangelical culture that frustrates him. And like Sunday School-age Nathan, the "edgy" author longs to be appreciated for transgression, admired for honesty, praised for courageous defiance. In his longing to be liked, he wants Facebook's "likes," as many as he can catch.

Now, don't get me wrong: I don't question the general drive for theological truth, for the public righting of perceived wrongs. But as Wiman puts it, "Truth inheres not in doctrine itself, but in the spirit with which it is engaged."[30] And, theological accuracy suspended, I sense, sizzling through cyberspace, shards of defiance like my mine. I sense selves formed in opposition to a culture, a Christian culture that frustrates but cannot be left, a culture masochistically cleaved to and disparaged all at once.

Of course, while Protestant culture has a long history of righteous insurrection (Could Luther's 95 Theses be considered the Internet Listicle's great-granddaddy?), these modern writings are also willing casualties of a media cycle that runs on outrage. "What X Gets Wrong About Y" is an oft-used headline template. It places writers one Mad Lib away from Clickbait gold. In June 2015, Indiewire published "The 10 Best Films of 2015 So Far According to the Criticwire Network, Plus 40 More." One week later, Indiewire published "Criticwire Survey: What Indiewire's Critics Poll Gets Wrong About the Best Movies of 2015 So Far,"[31] in which Indiewire *criticizes its own list.* This is the Internet culture in a nutshell: a culture of instantaneous scrutiny in which a website cannot even put forth a statement without throwing that same statement under the bus. Even when Indiewire creates a concrete list based on popular opinion, its desire is not to create a dialectical synthesis, to forge the sort of unity that Kierkegaard yearned for; its goal is to publish traffic-garnering content. Defiance garners traffic.

The defiant article even has a snazzy name: "The Hot Take," or, in a slightly more elevated mode, "The Think Piece." As Alissa Wilkinson explains in *Christianity Today*, The Hot Take almost always features:

> (1) a weak, quickly-made argument that is (2) written basically to garner lots of traffic. . . . The trick to writing on the Internet and getting heard is making a very loud, very extreme argument. The Internet does not reward nuanced takes or people who wait a week and a half to think something through, and the Internet *especially* does not reward people who say, *You know? I'm not sure I've figured out what I think on this yet.*[32]

The statement "What X gets Wrong About Y" demands an author's concrete, absolute understanding of right and wrong. Subjectivity and emotional nuance are utterly unwelcome. The author's "absolute understanding" is publicly flouted, defiantly obtruded upon a particular text or idea or person. The text or idea or person is perceived as a source of unjust power, one that is cleaved to out of malice and defiantly scrutinized. *You think you're powerful and so right, Most Christians/ Churches/Obama/Taylor Swift/Apple Inc./Jonathan Franzen/ Pope Francis/James Franco? Well here's what you get WRONG! Take THAT!*

The most frustrating problem with this tendency is that texts, ideas, and people are not limiting powers; they aren't Sunday School jailers; they throw no actual nets over our subjective thoughts. The Internet is a democratized space. But the cumulative deluge of external voices feels so much more *powerful* than our little, individual selves; we feel totally overwhelmed; it feels like the web's torrent of voices will drown us into insignificance. Our only desperate choice: rebel against the "Powers That Be."

So the real battle begins: pieces that are designed to defiantly assault the Powers That Be are, themselves, perceived as sources of crushing, suffocating power, and are taken to court in the dreaded Comments Section. In a recent *New Yorker* article, Mark O'Connell speaks for us all when he writes:

> If the Internet were to receive its own Ten Commandments—picture a Moses figure descending from Mountain View, clutching a stone phablet etched with a listicle of moral directives—somewhere in there would surely be the phrase "Thou Shalt Not Read the Comments." There are few online experiences more dispiriting, more arduously futile, than the downward scroll into the netherworld of half-assed provocations and inanities that exists beneath the typical opinion piece or YouTube video. It is plainly bad for the soul, the whole business, and yet we do it, all the time. . . .[33]

Yes, we do. I think we read the comments (or I read the comments, at least) because the Internet derives its specialized thrill from its mix of voices. Writers are no longer Singular Maestros; the media is no longer an omniscient System. We're all invited into the interpersonal fray. And yet, these articles, these perceived sources of power, are defied via gut reflex. The most critical comments are upvoted to the top of the list like the most popular, denim-clad rebels in the class. And so we're often left with giant, contradictory cleavages between defiant articles and defiant comments as perceived powers and defiant arguers begin to endlessly circle each other, because "the Internet itself, in all its incomprehensible vastness, [is] an exponentially ramifying network of commentary and metacommentary. It's comments all the way down."

In this space, the postmodern world is clearly not a world without truth-values. Quite the opposite: it's a world in which truth-values—didactic, revisionary, absolute, defiant—rest everywhere we look, in every comment and metacomment. (Except, perhaps, comments written by the so-called Internet "trolls," who—swiftly, undiscerningly, medievally—defy all of the moralistic defiance with their special brand of intentionally inane provocation.) A difference between the twenty-first century and the mid-twentieth century is that, now, there is no major split between two different sets of truth-values, between dominant culture and counterculture, establishment and underground, mainstream and avant-garde. As A. O. Scott analyzed in a smart piece, "Adjusting to a World That Won't Laugh With You," the twentieth century's rebel comedians (Flip Wilson, George Carlin, Joan Rivers, Richard Pryor) had actual power sources to defy. This made their defiance seem—to those wished to avoid the dreaded label "square"—palatable, even heroic: "What they were pushing against seemed self-evident, if also sometimes allegorical: the Man, the establishment, the agents of official centralized power." But now, even among, or particularly among, self-proclaimed liberals,

> We love jokes that find the far edge of the permissible, but we also love to turn against the joker who violates our own closely held taboos. In the blink of an eye, social media lights up not with twinkles of collective liking but with flames of righteous mob fury [because] contradictions have only multiplied, and the fantasy of an audience united in derision against unsmiling authority has tangled and frayed. Top-down censorship, applied by the state or cautious broadcasters, is a distant memory. . . . The Man is not going to tell us what we can or can't say, which means we have to tell each other . . .[34]

And yet: in a weird, dialectical way, the more Internet commenters brawl, the more alternative mediums grow in popularity—like podcasts, for instance. The podcast, as a form, almost fetishizes the art of genial, person-to-person conversation. *This American Life*'s podcast spinoff, *Serial*, became a breakout, multi-million-download hit not only because it dug deep into a real-life murder mystery but because its host, Sarah Koenig, has the remarkable capacity to host colloquial—even goofy!—conversations with possible murderers like Adnan Sayed and definitely-murderers like The Taliban. She does hard journalism about difficult issues and brings the rhetorical volume down to an incredibly sane level as she does it.

On podcasts, critics like Andy Greenwald and Chris Ryan turn into whip-fast screwball comics while actual comedians turn into stalwart truth seekers. Pete Holmes ends every conversation on *You Made It Weird* with a discussion about God—regardless of whether he's talking to Richard Rohr, Ray Romano, Rob Bell, or Sinbad. On *WTF*, Maron speaks tirelessly of his goal to escape the pull of solipsism in order to connect with others—even if (or *especially* if) he's talking to the President of the United States. These podcasts try to be the Internet's antidote to itself.

And yet, the more podcasts I listen to, the more I begin to pick up on a process that probably occurs in most non-recorded conversations, but one that's amplified by recording equipment: both talking partners instinctually lean toward points and occasions of mutual agreement despite their unspoken differences. You hear it when Pete Holmes subtly draws Keegan Michael-Key toward his ethereal, syncretic version of Liberal Christianity. You hear it when Adnan Sayed divulges his frustrations with Sarah Koenig via written letter because he can't voice them to her over the phone. You hear it when Maron's guests agree with his points before they've even processed what he's said to them. In moments like these, you can feel the desire for blasé connection, for simple unity, overwhelm our deeper desire for love in spite of difference or even because of difference. You feel a preference for what Martin Luther King Jr. called "a negative peace which is the absence of tension" rather than a "positive peace which is the presence of justice." Implied in that statement is something we often like to forget: tension can be good.

I've encountered one striking exception to the general blasé-connection/absence-of-tension vibe: Maron's conversation with his co-comedian and long-time friend (turned near-unfriend when the podcast was recorded) Louis C.K. *Slate* named their *WTF* conversation the "Greatest Podcast Episode Ever."

It begins with Maron's soft, tentative voice: "So, um. So, are we alright, me and you?"

"Yeah, sure."

Maron sighs and chuckles a little. "Okay."

"You mean personally?"

"Yeah."

"Ah, well, you know. We're under development, I think."

Maron brings up how Louis didn't reply to emails asking him to be on the podcast. Louis mentions how "I had time when I was writing you emails to connect with you personally, and you ignored me."

"Really?"

"Yeah, for a long time. For, I don't know. Over a year, longer than that."

"Ugh." Maron sighs.

"I would write emails and I'd say 'I'm not sure why you're not writing me back, but I'm gonna persist because our friendship goes back far enough and it's worth saving. You just wouldn't answer me. At some point I caught you on the phone and you said that when we talk it's just about me and I don't listen to you and I'm very self-centered, and I took that to heart—but I also thought, well, I felt like it was unfair. And after that I tried to pursue you and you still wouldn't talk to me."

By the end of the two-hour back-and-forth, they've talked about how Maron felt jealous of Louis's success, how that insecurity led him to push Louis away, how that made Louis feel: "If you see me doing something and you have a hard time coming to terms with it because of how you're feeling about your own life," he says, "what's really happening is you're letting me down as a friend. . . . I could've used yah. I got divorced. I had a show canceled, you know, I had some tough times. I could've used a friend."

Maron apologizes. Louis responds: "Well I apologize to you, because then I probably did it to you probably out of resentment. Ignored your emails because you ignored my phone calls back when there was no email."

Maron's voice, quiet, quivering: "Well can we get back on track or what?"

"Yeah," A short, significant pause. "I think we can."

It's brutal and beautiful. Immediately after listening, I sent a text to my Co-Programmer, now very good co-comedian friend, Henry. He doesn't like *WTF* very much, but I told him: "You *have* to listen to this episode." He did.

"Dude!" he texted me back. "*So* honest. Like, so damn open and honest. I only hope I can be that honest with a friend someday."

"Me too," I texted back. We didn't have an honest conversation about it, but we both hoped that we could be that honest with each other.

Most of the time, we'd rather be ourselves with all the agonies of hell than reach out in our states of vulnerable agony.

But sometimes, through conflict, through pain, through em-barrassment, an aperture might open up.

✶ ✶ ✶ ✶ ✶

Mr. Gleeson towered over children and he towered over normal-sized adults, too. He sported totems of the early 2000s: loose Hawaiian shirts, a prickly goatee, a slate gray PalmPilot. His piercing eyes squinted in a near-permanent look of detached, ironized contemplation, as if he was always smelling something funky but never something obscene. He was a deadpan grump, but a grump too removed from full-throttle sincerity to be intentionally cruel, and he was one of the few Sunday School teachers that I secretly admired be-cause he was as defiant as me.

Mr. Gleeson was my occasional Sunday School teacher, and, between fourth and sixth grades, my Wednesday night Beach Club small group leader. Mr. Gleeson never followed the Beach Club Coordinator's assigned curriculum. He never made us glue a single cotton ball sheep onto a single green sheet of construction paper. He would always complicate—and occasionally even contradict—the lesson taught to the large group before our small group broke off. We hardly read the Bible, and we never went through the numbered, pre-determined, mechanically precise questions. Instead, we did something unprecedentedly simple: we talked, about anything and everything, with satisfying openness because we knew that Mr. Gleeson was a stubborn, no BS guy. Puberty, mov-ies, poverty, breast cancer, weird sex stuff—it was all on the table. Mr. Gleeson offered take anyone in my fifth grade group with parental permission to see *The Passion of the Christ*. (I couldn't acquire parental permission.)

I asked Mr. Gleeson if he would teach my middle school and high school small groups. Mr. Gleeson said that he would apply, but the odds didn't look good. I didn't quite understand why; now I can only assume that his habit of stubborn impropriety was well-known. Mr. Gleeson was known for writing two-register scripts for various church events. Many of them went over my head. Just before my family moved to Texas, Mr. Gleeson wrote a skit for Dad's going away party. Through the grapevine, I learned that the skit had proved controversial, and, ultimately, subject to censorship, because it contained sly jokes about a dippy—albeit long-gone—congregant. This frustrated Mr. Gleeson as much as Ang frustrated me, perhaps even more so. Mr. Gleeson continues to write comedy scripts, but no longer for Irvine Presbyterian Church. He left.

Because I admired Mr. Gleeson's spirit of gutsy rebellion, I tempered my own defiance around him. And I experienced a nice shift: Schyler, a twitchy, anxious kid with long, scraggly hair, was now the one sent out into the hall for timeouts. I felt good. We were both on the same side, Mr. Gleeson and me, rebels with the same cause.

Or so I thought. And then came that one Sunday, in the middle of fifth grade, when Mr. Gleeson and Mrs. Taylor substitute taught a Sunday School class. (Or, more accurately, Mrs. Taylor did the teaching and Mr. Gleeson sat by the back wall.) I had a peculiar amount of energy that day; I don't remember why. (The first pings of testosterone?) So he took me aside and told me, quite simply, that if I did not behave he would walk me from the Jenny Hart Building across the patio, through the midsized, landscaped palm trees, into the gauzy windowed sanctuary, where he would interrupt my father's sermon in order to tell my father, in front of hundreds and hundreds of congregants, that I had been misbehaving in Sunday School.

I listened and nodded and returned to my seat, anything but threatened by such an utterly empty warning. He could have threatened something reasonable, at least! Mr. Gleeson was too sullen, too detached from Sunday School's misbehave-punishment routine to make good on these sorts of threats. He was too rebellious to punish rebellion.

Then, no more than fifteen energetic minutes later, Mr. Gleeson nodded at me across the room.

"Let's go."

As we left, I expected him to turn around to chat with me on a carpeted staircase, to maybe even engage in a little by-the-book Sunday School discipline with the typical "don't make me talk to your parents" warning. But we just kept going: down the purplish-brownish carpeted stairs, into the Jenny Hart Building's dark wood paneled hall. I couldn't figure out the game plan. When was he going to stop?

He didn't stop. He dutifully trudged onto the white, bright patio and my heart began to wrench and my head began to spin. *Oh God, it's really happening.* I was ambushed by adrenaline. I saw myself embarrassed, exposed in front of a pewed crowd that found my defiant jokes neither appropriate nor funny but shameful. I saw their frowns and their attempts to avoid eye contact, both uncomfortable themselves and uncomfortable on my behalf. I saw Dad speechless, caught off-guard, attempting to disarm the peculiarity of the situation with some of his much-beloved mid-sermon jokes. And most of all, I saw myself watching the whole church observing the rebel thrown under the bus by a rebel, the trickster tricked, the one-upper one-upped, unable to defend himself before this damning jury.

As Mr. Gleeson hopped up the white, grooved steps and approached the glass-doored narthex, he won. I broke down, full-on crying.

"Okay okay I'm sorry I'm sorry I'll stop I'll be good I'll be good I promise I'm sorry just stop okay? Just *stop*, okay I'm *sorry*. Alright. I'll be good. I promise."

Quick, punchy gasps in, mild moans out. Mr. Gleeson turned around, fixed his expressionless eyes on my tear-stained face. A pause. We walked back into the Jenny Hart Building, silent.

I told my mom what happened on our drive home from church. She was upset on my behalf. It wasn't a right punishment, it wasn't a fair punishment. It was a mean punishment. Not only would he not punish other kids like that; he couldn't *possibly* punish other kids like that. In turning the church culture against itself, he turned my unwitting position in the Church ecosystem against me. By cleaving to the system he so disliked, by exploiting it for his own advantage, he exploited me.

And on that day, I began to realize what defiance looked from the perspective of the defied. When Mr. Gleeson, the one so like me, turned his power against the system we both defied by turning on me, on my place within the system, I felt my own defiant spirit stabbing me in the chest. The proper Sunday School System, as much as it felt suffocatingly simple and irritatingly didactic, was also a system made of kind-but-firm punishment, hallway talking-tos, graciously tolerated Uncle Sam songs. To defy the Sunday School System entirely involved not only defying the behavioral structures imposed on me; it also involved defying the patience I was so often offered, the very patience—I began to realize—that I refused to offer my teachers.* There's a reason Kierkegaard calls the spirit of defiance not just a "stoic" spirit but a "demonic" spirit.

---

* Teachers, I now realize, who offered their free time to graciously put up with squirrely, disrespectful me. I trust my more-objective mom, a childhood development teacher, when I quote an email she sent after reading these chapters: "The main thing I think you got from your Sunday school years were adults who took an interest in you and tolerated your

Sometimes it takes a traumatic mirror to show you what you really look like.

✶ ✶ ✶ ✶ ✶

Despite the fact that I still have a Sunday School shard stuck in me, occasionally spurring me to angry action—like the time in high school when, during a particular harsh lecture from a Community Theater director, I stood up on my chair, hands literally quaking, and cried "YOU'RE NOT THE BOSS OF ME!!" before playing the dramatic explosion off as a joke—I am now particularly sensitive to, and generally avoidant of, the spirit of defiance in social life. I was once the wince-causer; now I wince.

Perhaps this is why it's so hard for me to engage Hot Takes with empathy or to read The Dreaded Comments with even-keeled blood pressure. I'm with A. O. Scott: "There is so much to be angry about, including the fact that people keep getting angry. . . . Can't we just all have a good time together?"[35]

Decontextualized, Scott's quote is a little misleading. Scott, like Kierkegaard, calls for something more like a dialectical synthesis. He concludes with a two-pronged conclusion—"laughter is something we should all take seriously. And also . . . we should all lighten up"—that seems equally critical and gracious—and necessary.

One night in New York in 2014, some friends who had studied in Prague with me encouraged me to participate in an Open Mic night at their favorite Alphabet City bar, the Revision Lounge and Gallery. I had done two standup sets in Prague during the fall after I worked at camp. The first was a smashing success; the second was a miserable failure—I

---

imagination—some were better than others. Makes me wonder how Sunday School could be better for little 'concrete' thinkers."

alienated my crowd with insensitive and sexually obscene jokes. (The Sunday School Shard pierced once again.) Every participant is given five minutes, my Prague friends told me—a longer allotment than many other bars in Manhattan allow. I agreed. I grabbed the best bits from my first set, put some observational material together, most of which I've forgotten,* and headed through a velvet curtain into a dark back room where a DJ desk fashioned from the front half of a Lincoln was parked in the back and a lonely, skinny microphone stood against a red brick wall.

All components of the Revision Lounge, including the bar itself, are made out of recycled materials. "Saved from the landfill," their website brags. So of course the lounge appeals to a demographic of young hipsters, and, just as predictably, most of the jokes that night felt self-consciously recycled. The crowded room was not only flooded with anti-humor, but with what felt like anti-*laughs*: laughs that seemed less like organic responses to genuine jokes than defiant responses to bad jokes, laughs laughed *in spite of* unfunny jokes. On the night I performed, the room was so crowded that each participant's allotted time was cut down to two minutes, and, later, ninety seconds. On a dirty velvet couch in the back right corner, I peered at my scribbled notes in the dark, trying less to determine what to cut than what to save from my landfill of prepared material.

Ninety seconds gives a comedian almost no time to establish an interpersonal connection with her audience. There's no opportunity for back-and-forth. It's barely enough time to barrage the audience with your defiant comments, your

---

* Notes still sit in my iPhone like lines of mediocre poetry: "thesis paragraph bit/context clues, twitter, how to read irony/guy hating on twitter, think he's sincere/computer sex thing."

half-assed provocations and inanities, like most of the comedians did that night—either flailing, speed-talking for a
couple laughs, or reflexively building off of the insane task
of pulling laughs from a crowd of self-involved hipsters. (It
seemed like every person there performed. And, like me, everyone seemed more preoccupied with their own material
than with their mediocre onstage peers.) I tried the flailing
tactic. I felt a rush of stress as I tried to defy the jaded mass:
*come on like me, laugh at me, come on, I worked on this stuff,
it's good, I'm funny!* I got a few laughs, and mostly silence,
before I left the stage and breathed a sigh of relief.

The night's spirit was best expressed by a chunky guy
with a stringy beard and a faded T-shirt. He came up and
announced that it was his birthday. Little claps. He went on
with a bit that received a couple half-hearted laughs before he
arrived at his climax: "I've been married for five years. I actually met my girlfriend during 9/11 when we left New York and
went down to Philly. It turns out that that an end of the world
apocalypse can get you laid." Silence. The defiant comedian
in me began to read the situation . . . *come on man, don't say
it, don't say it, don't say it!* He said it. "As those towers were
falling down, my tower was popping up!" Genuine groans
spread all over the room, the most genuine releases I heard
that night. He looked around, glumly: "Awe, come on guys,
it's my birthday! You guys suck." He put the mic down and left
the stage, dejected. One or two scattered claps followed him
through the velvet curtain into the bar, where he inevitably
nursed down something strong and terrible.

It's hard to be sure if the birthday bit at the end was
planned, but I suspect so. As the night sits in my uncomfortable memory, the planned-birthday bit was perhaps the sad-
dest bit of all because it was a sign of rejection *prepared for*, of
failure worked into the set itself and thrown onto the audience

out of self-defense, as if *it* was the one who screwed up. When my Prague set bombed, I only blamed my audience in my head; I didn't attack them right then and there. But of course I wouldn't blame them publicly because I knew they wouldn't like that and then they wouldn't like me. So was this comedian expecting us to masochistically enjoy him for his verbal attack? Maybe. Or else that final line was a cry in the dark, in the most desolate sense of that phrase. The poor comedian had already defied so much: standards of taste, respect, not to mention the expectation that he'd actually have funny material. So he ended by defying the one thing he actually wanted: his own desire to be liked for transgression. He gave up on the possibility of any sort of connection, even a connection built on anti-humor's shared irony. He held tightly to "something the Christian would call a cross, a basic defect," as he sunk to the bottom of his defiant pain. "To seek help from someone else—no, not for all the world does he want that. Rather than to seek help, he prefers, if necessary, to be himself with all the agonies of hell."

And yet, I kind of admire the guy for his courage. He merely vocalized the defiant sadness I felt in that room. How many other would-be comedians would've liked to shout "You guys suck!" that night? How many others wanted to be liked for their standup and were left wanting?

Even the anti-comedians couldn't mask that whiff. It's not so much that the anti-comedian has a split personality so much as it has a self in constant, mutating states of dissatisfaction—a self that performs comedy in order to be liked by others, but then a self that pushes others away because it thinks the connection will fail, or that the connection will be forged out of the shared sense of a failed set. The anti-comedian defies loneliness, then open-armed connection, then loneliness, then connection, until it finally gives up comedy all together. It's the self that cries into the void until it loses any voice it once had.

Perhaps I just came in on a bad night or perhaps it was a poor venue. Surely not all open mic nights are sites of existential despair-in-the-making? Or perhaps they are. As Louis C.K. recently told Terry Gross: "People that start doing standup are very crazy. You know, they really want it so badly. It's a very deep desire. And when you start, you stink. There's no other way to do it. It takes some kind of mental illness to push against that, you know, to go onstage and bomb horribly . . ."[36]

Louie, which Louis C.K. writes, directs, and edits, is as profane as *Veep,* but it takes on a calmer, more contemplative perspective. On *Louie,* defiance is not a response to the oppressive D.C. pressure cooker. It's a response to an emptiness felt at the heart of life itself—an emptiness that makes revolt seem less funny than soul-crushingly sad.

On *Louie,* C.K.'s fictional persona runs into a pudgy, middle-aged guy with coarse black stubble and a black beanie and sad wet eyes like a dog. This is Eddie, who had been a mentor to Louie. The two started doing comedy together at the same time. After Young Louie stunk on stage, Eddie told Louie: "You don't suck. They suck. Don't let other people tell you who you are, man. Don't do that. You're good. You're funny," and whacked him. *Awe, come on guys, it's my birthday! You guys suck.*

Eddie confronts everyone he meets. Does he work out of LA? "Oh yeah, because if I don't work in New York I have to work in LA. You know, there's a whole middle of the country. You know, the sewers of America? That's where I work. Places you wouldn't be welcome, phony New York piece of . . ." To the ethnic cashier at a liquor store: "Why don't you shut your hummus hole there, curry monkey? One star for your bar!"

He takes money from the tip jar. He spits vodka onto the liquor store window.

Eddie wants to do a set, but he doesn't want to go to a comedy club. "That's where comedy goes to die. Let's do an open mic."

Louie and Eddie drive off to Brooklyn, drinking vodka out of the bottle. They head into a dark room with a lone mic against a red brick wall before a dead audience. Open Mic-ers pause for laughs anyway. Eddie and Louie peer into the dark. Eddie whispers: "This is an open mic. Smell the desperation . . . it's just, it's just . . . loserdom." Eddie wanders on the stage, wild eyed, sweat glistening, smiling maniacally: "Your host, everyone. Give it up. He should."

Eddie leaves with Louie after his set. Eddie says that Louie should live in Brooklyn instead of Manhattan. Louie is defensive. "I used to live here, man. I lived in a five-floor walkup for two years with my ex-wife. The Twin Towers were right across the river. She was six months pregnant and we stood there and watched them burn."

"You just stood there and watched them burn? You didn't try to help, rush in, try to blow it up? Nothing? Come on, help three thousand brothas out, man. Stand there and watch them burn with your fattened wife who you later abandoned . . ."

"What's your deal, man?"

"I know we've burned our bridges and all that, but I've got no bridges left. I've burned bridges, I've burned roads, I've burned trails, I've burned the hiking path. . . . I'm cashin' in. I'm done. I'm forty shit years old, I've got nothing, I've got nobody, and I don't *want* anything. I don't *want* anybody. And that's the worst part, when the want goes, that's bad. Suffering is one thing, not having is one thing, but when you don't care anymore. . . . You get to the time when you think maybe it's time to put a period at the end of whatever this was."

"So you're gonna quit comedy."

". . . My life. I'm going to end it."

Louie stares intently, angrily, eyes electric: "You can't kill yourself."

Eddie asks for one good reason why he "can't."

Louie fumbles around before spewing: "You know what, it's not your life. It's life. Life is bigger than you, if you can imagine that. Life isn't something that you possess. It's something that you take part in and witness."

And here, a bit of Louis C.K. himself, the comedian who's been compared to Pascal, Augustine, Kant, Kierkegaard, Sartre, Camus, Heidegger, "practices" what Zadie Smith aptly calls "his comedy-cum-art-cum-philosophy."[37] The whole episode resonates because it's not just a struggle between C.K. and his earlier comedic mentor. It's a struggle between C.K. and the early comedic self that defied failure by shielding himself from the audience that rejected him. *You don't suck. They suck.* In Eddie, C.K. sees his early comedic defiance, that open-miced spirit of indignant desperation, after it's metastasized into the entire void of a life about to end. September 11 no longer matters to Eddie because life no longer matters to him. Bridges between people, mediums between people, don't matter to Eddie anymore; he's burned them all. Eddie hardly cares if he dies because, like Mrs. May in Flannery O'Connor's story "Greenleaf," he already lives in the Hell he's made for himself.

Except: "It's not your life. It's life. Life is bigger than you, if you can imagine that. Life isn't something that you possess. It's something that you take part in and witness." Here we see Louie as a growing comedian. This line is a hint of the wildly popular Louis C.K. we know today, the comedian who feels less like a defiant joke slinger than a profane, secular preacher, a charitable provider of mass exformation, a vessel for interpersonal growth, a shining beacon of what comedy can be: a medium that tenderly guides a collective will surging toward mutually felt truth. *It's not your life. It's not something you possess.* As the cliché puts it, "Life is a gift." And as Kierkegaard puts it, "through the aid of the eternal the self has the courage to lose itself in order to win itself." The self that has the courage to dispossess its own ego—what a radical notion, in this age of defiance!

I knew these ideas, theoretically, in May 2014. I was a self-proclaimed Christian by then. I listened to Tim Keller every Sunday. I no longer needed Mr. Gleeson's mirror; Facebook and Twitter were Eddie to me, always showing me what I could become, what I often was, what I often am, despite my best intentions. But the longer I sat in that dark, defiant room, the more I actually *felt* the weight of that suffocating, limiting, deadly spirit—a spirit more suffocating, limiting, deadly, than any spirit I ever felt in Sunday School—and the less I wanted improve my set, the less I wanted to beat the system from inside the system, and the more I longed to *know* those desperate would-be-comedians the more I longed to break through their defiant jackass shields. The more I wanted to leave my defiant will at Revision's landfill.

I walked out of Revision into a warm summer rain and never returned. I revised.

PART TWO

A lofty passage does not convince the reason of
the reader, but takes him **out of himself**.

Longinus, *On The Sublime*

Definitely Candid and Not Posed by Wannabe Bigshot Auteur, February 6, 2009

CHAPTER 4

FILM

Applause met me on the Boerne Community Theater stage. I was wearing a used tweed jacket with suede-patched elbows and a striped black button-up tucked into tight olive green pants. The outfit might've looked a little superficial on a high school senior, a little faux-trendy-intellectual for Central Texas, but I meant it: there were people from church, school, camp, and the theater community taking time out of the Christmas season and they deserved me at my best. I also meant it when I sliced my fingertips at my neck and shook my head and mouthed "no, no" at the sixty people clapping in their leather burgundy seats—I was premiering a short, the first serious film of mine they'd seen; it felt weird to receive their gracious affection right off the bat; I didn't deserve it yet—but then they thought I was goading their applause by making an exaggerated show of cutting it off. They thought it was self-centered camp so they laughed.

That was a bit of failed seriousness. The seriousness of the evening did not fail, though. Steven Parra's cotton outdoor screen, with its wrinkled surface stretched out on a PVC frame, fit into the little theater just right. Wires dangling from the sound booth hooked my Macbook into the system and hooked the crowd into *Sacrifice,* the seven-minute short I made for film school submissions. We watched it once at the beginning of the evening, once at the end, with an actor interview and a Q&A sandwiched in the middle.

I discovered the unique pleasure that came from standing tall on the stage to publicly thank my volunteer actors and helpers: Pastor John Watson as Old Man Jackson, tied to an oak tree with dirt rubbed onto his face as the film begins, about to take a shotgun round to the chest by Craig Childs; Austin Yount as the young man who slips out of his own ropes, dives in front of the bullet, and dies*; Mr. Yoder, totally willing to take direction from eighteen-year-old me and memorize paragraphs of wordy dialogue without a qualm. He recites monologues in a dark blue suit and leather business shoes at a desk—the heavy desk that Steven and Kara helped me carry into a creek in the canyon on Craig's ranch at five o'clock on an early August morning.

That was the best part of the evening, the thanksgiving. Either that or the Q&A, which I scheduled for thirty minutes

---

* Austin was willing to fall and spit-take watered-down marinara sauce onto grass for take after take. He didn't eat spaghetti for months afterward.

but stretched into a full hour because people were so engaged with the issues at hand. We broke down the line between entertainer and entertained so thoroughly that I ended up responding to audience members with my own questions and audience members asked audience members questions and it felt like the best sort of philosophy seminar: you could feel the fizzle of cognitive energy zipping around the room from one node to another, so many different minds clasped in a wild hunt for truth with my experiment guiding them.

The film was an ambiguous ethical parable, a riff on "The Grand Inquisitor," the story my dad mentioned in a small group he led for me and my friends and which I pretended to know about in order to impress a smart girl named Monica at Starbucks, but which I hadn't read. After the young man dies, he joins Mr. Yoder's tan, business-attired mystery man at the desk in the middle of the creek. The young man, goaded by this sly, pompous Inquisitor, claims that he gave his life because it was the right thing to do. The Inquisitor responds as cicadas hiss: "It's a great idea, isn't it? That there's some standard making things black and white, good and bad. What a good defense mechanism!" The real reason for his sacrifice, the Inquisitor claims, is that he wanted to go to heaven; he "wanted *honor*, for doing the best of the best." He should find other outlets for self-righteous satisfaction like homeless feeding. The Inquisitor claims he's telling him this because the Inquisitor keeps the world running; the Inquisitor "keeps the rich rich and the poor poor." So the Inquisitor allows one more shot and, in the film's last couple shots, we return to its opening shot. The shotgun is loaded again. The old man's face is ashen again. But the young man's hands lie limp in his ropes this time. He looks hesitant—until, yet again, he slips out and runs and and dies, with a laugh and a knowing smile this time.

What made the young man change his mind? Did he do the right thing? We learn that he has a baby on the way, after all. Was the Inquisitor's argument convincing—yes, no, somewhat? We had a lot to talk about in the community theater. And watching the film now, I kind of admire its lean, wiry guts, even if too much of the middle just cuts around the desk in four static medium shots and even though it so clearly reifies the mind of a kid that just needed to go to college and get his brain blown up and even though the dialogue feels portentous and overwrought. ("The intellectual nature of the conversation is part of the Inquisitor's intimidation strategy!" old me would say to current me. Fair enough, but, intellection doesn't make for great visual *cinema,* man, and lines like "Why so determinately give yourself up?" and "So it was a reflex of altruism, huh? Appealing to the Moral Law?" and— oy vey—"If you only knew that the superego was a moralistic perversion of the id, wrapping itself up in the pretty disguise of altruism!" feel both wooden *and* slightly showoffy.) No wonder it bored the USC film school admissions crew.

And yet, if the film still kinda works, it's because its heavy ideas are cushioned, if not lifted up, by elements that had less to do with my brain-in-the-making. There are the sharp green yucca swords radiating from the stem into the first establishing shot, the glen with slender oaks shooting out of bright green tropical grass, smoke rising from the shotgun chamber as the shell flies out, rich red blood on the bright green grass. Then, after a fade, the dollop of hanging moss dripping as Austin wakes up by the canyon wall; the blob of dried wax from the flickering candle on the desk lit by purple sunrise; the bright canyon wall blown-out by later light; the silt swirling on the surface of the creek and swirling, by extension, the surface of screen.

I don't wish to make some brash distinction between fine form and so-so content, though. As Sontag so emphatically argues in her essay "On Style," "form" and "content" can't be so easily parsed; form isn't like an Instagram filter applied to some otherwise-pure shard of consciousness; form pierces through all levels of a work like a watermark. Or maybe that's too violent an analogy: it's not like physical form pierces through the ideas undergirding *Sacrifice* like a shotgun blast to the chest. It's like the form of the world took my ideas into itself. It wrapped itself around them; it knit itself to them. It graced them with beauty and a sensuous significance that still pour forth onto every screen it fills.

In an interview from the Summer 2014 issue of *Bomb Magazine*, Giuliana Bruno was asked about her new release, a book called *Surface: Matters of Aesthetics, Materiality, and Media*. "There is a tendency in our culture to denigrate surfaces," she says. "People say something is superficial when they want to put it down. But, in fact, surface matters. Its so sensual and central to our lives."[38]

I like that word, "surface." It's similar to the other word I've already used, "image," in the sense that it can function as a pejorative. It can describe a lack: the argument or book or film "barely scratches the surface"; it's a "surface level" effort or even "surfacey." During the summer after my sophomore year of high school, after I saw *Fargo* for the first time and I felt like it threw my mind in a wood chipper in the best way possible (never before had I seen a neo-*noir*, nor any movie so region-specific and character-centric and funny and cynical and sweet and all at once), I wrote the script for a film called *Beneath the Surface*. The central image in my mind, the first shot as the open credits would roll: the camera looks up from the bottom of my pool at an elongated shape taped inside a couple Hefty trash bags, sinking. The title had a double meaning, of course: it also referred to the sinister underbelly of the small Texas town that, as in *Fargo*, would turn belly up when the teenage son of the local police chief would wake up to find the result of a mob murder gone wrong lying limp at the bottom of his family pool. Beneath the shallow surface of Texas Nice, the deeper truth would lie.

But "surface" can also describe a positive development: new evidence has surfaced; truth rises to the surface, just as it rises when the teenage protagonist jumps into his pool and lifts up what just so happens to be a corpse. A surface isn't just part of the thing; it's also the space where revelation occurs. This is seems to be Bruno's thesis, or part of the general thrust behind her book, at least:

> I wanted to think about the surface as a place of connection, as a meeting place . . . it mediates between inside and outside, and that mediation is also a form of projection. Film was invented and, at the same time, projection was defined by Freud as a psychic mechanism that regulates the boundaries between subjects and objects, and mediates the transfer between what we perceive as internal or external. I find it very interesting when artists use projection in a way that questions this idea of inside and outside—so that the screen as a surface becomes this place of transfer where you can really project affect, project mental space. . . .

Surface as a place of connection, a meeting place . . . this makes me think of the family friend who wished to Skype with me, the wording he used: "I can't miss this opportunity to break bread . . . even via Skype!" Skype is an imperfect surface, he knows, but even Skype presents the opportunity for some type of connection, some sort of communion. He is also a black man writing to me in a summer ripe with racial tension and all sorts of didactic online posturing. His consistent urge, post after post, is that we "set tables": "Fact, Facebook is great, as a tool, classrooms are fantastic to learn in. But, getting up, stepping out, asking questions, and sitting at a table and breaking bread with someone who doesn't look, sound, or act like you is what this country needs most of all. And Christ taught that lesson years ago with his disciples." Isn't the table the quintessential flat surface, the quintessential meeting place, too?

Revelations vary by degree, though. But that's one of the benefits of the term "surface." The term "image" evokes "only part of a thing," that infuriating illusion of presence, the cavity that lies between visible objectivity and hidden subjectivity. Surfaces, on the other hand, can be *touched*. "Feel the holes in my hands" said the resurrected Christ, revealing himself with far more intimacy than a mere image could provide. He wasn't a mere ghost, an image-without-presence. Bruno writes what I'd like to believe:

> We cannot really comprehend space by *looking* alone. By shifting away from this notion that we understand a canvas, or architecture, or cinema by way of looking only, I want to emphasize a haptic mode of art reception, a more relational mode derived from the sense of touch that surfaces convey. The reciprocal con*tact* between us and objects or environments occurs on the surface, in close encounters with art objects. As forms of materiality that touch us and can be touched, surfaces affect us.

✶ ✶ ✶ ✶ ✶

As much as I clearly love cinema as a medium, I don't think I ever really loved film before I knew it as a haptic medium, as something I could intimately manipulate, touch. Films were certainly more exciting than flannelgraphs, but—homes of Big

Guys, Captain Hooks, Child Snatchers—they imposed themselves on my mind in the same annihilating fashion. I was a bigger fan of drawing, making up stories with my guys, and, when I learned how to do it, writing. I wrote my first piece of fiction in kindergarten: *Johnny Thunder and the Lost Robe* [sic]. The plot, as far as I can recall, charted the quest of Johnny Thunder—an Indiana Jones knockoff created by The Lego Group before they started snagging licensed Lucasfilm characters—as he and his trusty steed overcame various obstacles in search of the eponymous Lost Ruby. Mrs. Bryant was kind enough to let me read portions of the book in regular installments during Share Time. I worked on the novel for weeks and weeks, writing text and drawing illustrations with fat Crayola markers on my drawing table, at the kitchen table, in the car until I ended up car sick. It was so fun. And so I decided, sometime between first and second grade, that I wanted to be an author.

All of this changed on the day, in third grade, when Dad presented a video of first-grade Kara's performance of Wendy in an after school acting class production of *Peter Pan*. He brought it downstairs on videotape, but it began with a black screen. And then the colorful title faded in: "A Roberts Family Production." It faded out . . . and another arrived, with spinning text this time: "Starring Kara Roberts as Wendy."

The video itself was a straightforward camcordered performance—just Kara singing whatever song Wendy sings in the show—but the applause was enhanced by a sound effect that continued as the last title slide appeared in a different font: "The End."

I had never seen an iMovie production. The titles and applause filled me with a sense of flushed excitement, just like when I'd hover over those sheets of white paper, fat marker in hand, invited to create. *That was like a* real *movie,* I thought. *We can make real movies!*

Two years later: A boy in a black zip-up sweatshirt is a very mysterious man with an exaggerated slouch, walking ever so slowly, hiding his face in his hood bent over a walking stick that's almost as tall as he is. Leafy tropical trees rise over his head. (Tropical bird sound effect, pattering-rain-on-waxy-leaves sound effect.) We pan along and keep our distance but stay firmly above the waist.

A voiceover—prepubescent and drawn out, heightened, deepened, pumped full of gravitas: "A looonnnggg time ago, the wizards and wise ones said that there would once be a most . . . *unexpected* hero." The mysterious man turns toward us, showing the dead-serious expression of a first-time *auteur*.

We pan out, fast! He's standing in backyard grass; he twirls the walking stick into the shrubbery on his right like a massive baton and a glass breaking sound effect plays as it lands and he throws the sweatshirt open and thrusts his now-free arm in the air, revealing a pudgy tummy above saggy blue briefs and pasty white thighs.

The voiceover is incredulous: "Ummmm. . . . That's him in the underpants."

The Simpsons theme song plays over comic sans titles: "From The Maker of Henry Billy Joe Sausage ['That was . . . a little comic strip I drew while bored in fifth grade class?] and Happy Idiots [I just don't know], comes a movie that will make you beg for change!"

Cut to the Mysterious Man sitting on a brick patio against the back wall of a house in his open sweatshirt and briefs.* Love handles ripple and little man boobs poke out like mole noses. He uses one hand to hide his crotch with a towel; he

---

* The only sensory memory I have from this whole production: how cold the brick was against my lower thigh, how much comfort I had to sacrifice for the *art*!

holds a plastic Spiderman cup in the other. A towering figure in off-white capris and a Batman mask with a black drape enters the frame.* The Mysterious Man's voice is broken, gravelly, old: "Change. . . . A little change for the homeless. . . . Chaaannngge." The Batman-type-figure has a British accent. "You *loser!*" (s)he says as (s)he rears up and fakes a giant loogie hawk and propels a big ol' spit. He drops the cup and jumps up and says in a strong, deep-ish voice: "You're messing with the wrong robo—eh, wrong hobo, man!"

"Oh yeah?!"

"Yeah!!"

He swings an exaggerated uppercut to the face and it's met with a giant punch sound effect and there's irregular senseless grunting from both of them as he jabs Batman-type's shoulder and pushes and punches and pushes. He grabs both shoulders and pulls down. "Yeeeuhh!" He jabs at the small of Batman-type's back as Batman-type hits the brick. Butt-cheek outlines grace the camera as he flings his arms downward. Batman-type whimpers in a fetal position. He puts one bent, pasty leg on Batman-type's *teres major* and puts up his dukes. His strawberry blond hair is steaked back, windswept.

"That's what I'm talking about."

Yellow hand-scribbled-looking text drops and the voice-over cries: "Hobos United!"

The *Mission Impossible* theme plays and the Mysterious Man charges into a bedroom in a half-crouch that's supposed to be sneaky, I guess, and he jumps on the queen-sized bed and rolls over in horizontal spins, flashing bits of flab until he drops off the other side and Homer Simpson cries "Doh!" and

---

* The character was supposed to be a wealthy aristocrat, but, as Beth recently told me: "I don't think I knew what you were trying to do. You probably didn't explain yourself very well." I'm sure she's right.

a big thump sound effect plays as he hits the ground offscreen. The final title flashes: "Friday, December 5."

This was the first film I ever made.

I'm not sure how developed the full *Hobos United* concept was when I enlisted Beth's help to make this trailer. But like most sitcom pilots, it contained the germ of an idea, perhaps the core of the idea. Rewatching it, I gawk at my pre-cooked sugar cookie of a body and wonder why capris were ever in style: I also gawk at its cinematic language and visual humor: the dramatic build-up and the comedic reversal, the shocking reveal of layered punch lines, the balance between what is shown and not shown in any particular shot, the pairing of audio and video (jungle sounds: good for dramatic mystery; *The Simpsons* theme song: perfect for loopy comedy). This isn't to say that I was some cinematographic savant or something, but it is to say that I exhibited what I've noticed in videos people made when the Vine app was popular: we've all learned cinematic language by immersion. Without lessons we know how to communicate, how to affect others, how to draw people in. The *Hobos United* trailer is rudimentary, but all the component parts are there.

I started to build the component parts into a full-on machine. The storyline was simple, archetypical: a group of hobos (Why "hobo" and not "homeless"? *You* tell *me* what word is funnier), tired of being disrespected and beat on by the snotty upper crust, join together for retribution and justice. They form a vigilante team. In true superhero style, they're named after their "particular set of hobo skills," as Liam Neeson would put it, names like The Cart Crasher (he crashes into people with shopping carts) and The Bag Basher (he wields a full Hefty trash bag as a massive mace).

I cast my friends as individual heroes and began to make more trailers. My favorite no longer exists, as far as I know, but the opening shot is burned into my inner eye. It's a wide shot in the parking lot behind Ralphs supermarket. Something's coming toward us in the distance. The *2001: A Space Odyssey* theme begins, softly, getting louder, full of weight and suspense and burgeoning significance. Then we begin to discern: a hobo (me) wearing a mustard yellow shirt full of big swiss-cheese holes, navigating the asphalt ocean in his shopping cart vessel, using his wooden staff as an oar.

He draws closer, closer, closer as the music builds, builds, builds until we discover his target: a yuppie in a buttoned-up shirt and clip-on tie, whom he pulls up alongside and repeatedly hits with the walking stick! Whacking sound effect after whacking sound effect! The yuppie falls to the ground. (My poor friend Ben, kind enough to play this yuppie, was a victim of my method acting.) It was the most work I had ever done on a film, ripping up the old shirt, putting Ben in costume, convincing him to get whacked with my staff, convincing another babysitter, Laurie, to drive us to Ralphs to film the darn thing, snagging the cart, navigating the uneven lot in that rickety metal vessel. Finding the *2001* theme—so broad, tense, portentous—was a godsend. As I edited the trailer, it felt like an electric current ran up and down my body. I rubbed my hands together just to let the energy out.

It's tempting, and perhaps somewhat true, to suggest that I was so excited because this represented some late stage in a process of artistic evolution. With every developmental step I was bringing the outer world further and further into my inner world, strengthening my sense of self, developing, like Edward Hopper, "imaginative ownership and psychic freedom." With drawings, I could take imaginative ownership of life's jungles. When writing, I could cement and share the sorts of narratives I created with my guys—narratives of jungle exploration, heroes boldly searching for lost rubies.

And with "professional" live action movies, I could bring real people, real places, under my creative control.

This sort of control underlies the conception of the great cinematic *auteur*. Hitchcock, Bergman, Fellini, Godard, Truffaut, Antonioni, Kubrick, Tarkovsky, De Palma, Herzog, Scorsese, Lynch: these directors are regarded because of their supposed capacity to bring every *mise-en-scène*, every performance, every soundtrack, every edit, every color correction, every everything under their creative control. Think Kubrick forcing poor Shelley Duvall to perform take after take for *The Shining*, pushing her toward a state of literal hysteria for his authorial benefit. Think Herzog moving a real 340-ton steamship over a mountain for *Fitzcarraldo*. Think Wes Anderson's precise aspect ratios, ceaseless symmetry, careful patterns, quirky knick-knacks. In an interview for the *New York Times*, Anderson's longtime cinematographer Robert Yeoman said: "You could be standing on top of a mountain, and you'd still see some of the signature motifs. That's just how Wes sees the world."[39] *That's just how Wes sees the world*: the whole world is subsumed by Anderson's subjective vision.

The auteur theory is appealing because it easily explains the appeal of the cinematic medium. "More than any other medium," Joe Cinephile might say, "film gives you the opportunity to see and hear the entire world as someone else sees it." A film viewer sees the same thing the auteur saw when she looked through the viewfinder. Film is the manifestation of the auteur's consciousness—the external projection of her internal state, the site "where you can really project affect, project mental space." In his book *In The Blink of An Eye*, Francis Ford Coppola's longtime editor Walter Murch makes a compelling argument that good film edits even align with the emotional rhythm of our literal blinks. They make us blink when the auteur blinks. And therefore, when we watch films, we get to empathize with the filmmakers' worldview, even, or especially, if it's different than our own.

I like this argument because it's neat and often true. But at the same time, when I think about the films I've made, the films I love, I'm not sure if it's sufficient.

One of this theory's weaknesses is that in fiction, we don't just demand a director's subjectivity. We want our directors to have compassion for characters, too. In a truly great film, multiple levels of sympathy overlap. One of my most surprising recent experiences with multiple sympathy levels occurred while watching Harmony Korine's *Spring Breakers*. I went to see *Spring Breakers* during sophomore year of college because critics liked it and my friends liked it. But I was skeptical. The überhedonistic college beach party culture that lies at its pulsing, Skrillex-pumped heart is the kind of culture I do my best to avoid. Never mind my own occasional lapses into King Solomonesque excess: how sensual, how vapid, how *stupid* it is. Leave me out.

Spring Breakers propels us into a world of immediate, hypnotic, perpetual motion. Some of the shots, appropriated from *Girls Gone Wild*, are just plain gross. They made my heart churn and writhe. And yet . . . as the titular spring breakers relish in beer poured across naked bodies, as liquor is poured into open mouths, as girls suck red-white-and-blue popsicles, as the sublime Florida sun graces gyrating bodies and the cool salt water licks their spray-tanned skin, it's . . . beautiful. Not ethically, not narratively, not thematically, no, but, visually, it's jaw-dropping. *Is this a form of irony?* I first thought, *the distance between this beautiful façade and the horrid substance?*

Well . . . maybe. Then I started changing my mind. The form and the substance still seem inseparably linked, somehow. There seems to be a different method to this madness. By the

time it ended, I believed that Korine's film doesn't run on
irony, but on a form of cinematic empathy that astonishes
with its sensual immediacy. The camera swings along, pushing here and pulling there, immersing the audience in a sea
of color and stylistic excess. Juxtapositions create a sense of
life, motion, an intensity of feeling. Korine is so enthusiastic
to immerse you in the world that he takes your breath away
with a peculiar mixture of delight and disgust. The neons are
green, pink, vivid; the sunsets are goldenrod yellow; the water
sparkles. It's almost heavenly . . . *just as its main characters
wish it to be.*

German Expressionism is a movement in early film history with a defining characteristic: expressionist films project
their characters' internal states-of-mind onto their external
environments, shaping and revealing them through shot com-
position. Subjectivity rises to the surface, externalized. These
characteristics are most recognizable to Americans as revived
though American film noir in the 1940s: canted angles illu-
minate a world that feels out of whack; fog implies a world of
mysteries and hidden truths; bleak cities express moral bleak-
ness; shadows from venetian blinds look like shadows from
prison bars knocked horizontal, and so on.

But it seems to me that some of the most moving films exhibit expressionist tendencies. *Spring Breakers* is one of them.
One of its central characters, Faith, is a young Christian who
decides to spend a week substituting the Holy Spirit, her usual
intoxicant, for a plethora of others. On the phone with her
grandma she says, without irony: "This is the most spiritual
place I've ever been." Because I saw this world as she's seen
it—pulsing, swirling, intoxicating—I believed her. I might not
touch March in St. Petersburg with a multi-hundred-mile-
long pole, but I understood, briefly, why college students head
there on pilgrimage. I felt, just a bit, just enough, what they

feel, because I saw it as they saw it. We shared a slight, tenuous link between our minds, mediated by Korine's luxurious screen. He opened his camera up to externalize a worldview that's often chided. He took it seriously. He hit on the spiritual longing that underlies what Kierkegaard would call the Aesthetic Life and it hit my soul like a gong.

I love that famous quote by the playwright Terence: "I am human: nothing human is alien to me,"* but it would be too vain for me to say with complete honesty: many humans *are* alien to me, and I need brave artists like Harmony Korine to—if not *translate* alien customs, exactly—open up shared visions, lines of sight, spatial perspectives. By the time the extreme debauchery triggers extreme consequences for its central characters,† and by the time our prodigals' possible return glimmers like a far-off sun sunset on the gulf coast, I found myself—in perhaps the dirtiest, grossest film I'd ever seen, mind you—full-on crying in the Regal Union Square. In an auditorium full of cultured Manhattanites, I felt like a freak. The culmination of sympathy and wisdom (Korine's and, suddenly, mine), the surprise shock of unprecedented understanding, and a deep longing for these young peoples' spiritual thirst to be quenched rather than numbed by the endless hunger of a violent hangover, did me in. I felt simultaneously, paradoxically, pulled out of myself and personally nourished. Even when Ellie Goulding's club song "Lights"

---

* Here I'm using the quote as written as an epigram in Leslie Jamison's *The Empathy Exams*. It's from *The Self-Tormenter,* but I'm not sure what translation or edition it's taken from.

† And that's the dramatic key to *Spring Breakers*, perhaps: while it's full of sympathy for its hedonists, the narrative evokes a classic, Aristotelian sense of cause and effect, sin and logical consequence. The aesthetic is sympathetically permissive, but the narrative is unsentimentally grounded.

played over the credits, its lyrics seemed to portray a post-
traumatic subjectivity: "And I'm not sleeping now, the dark
is too hard to beat/And I'm not keeping now, the strength I
need to push me."

Not everyone saw *Spring Breakers* the way I did. Young
men were probably turned on. Conservatives were offended.
I heard somewhere that real spring breakers didn't like it because it threw their lives in a funhouse mirror. Others liked
it, but assumed that Korine was being ironic. In a culture fu-
eled by equal doses of irony and defiance, that's an easy assumption to make. It's easy to assume that his seriousness
must be faux-seriousness marshaled for the sake of a massive joke: "He *can't* be taking these people seriously. He can't
really treat them like they're as young and beautiful and alive
as they think they are." And yet, except for some classically
ironic slippages here and there (like a [nevertheless sublime]
sing-along dance routine to Brittney Spears' "Everytime" performed with bikinis and ski masks and shotguns), Korine's
irony feels . . . unusual. More sincere than corrosive. More
true than cruel. Perhaps he's working from the German film
critic Siegfried Kracauer's mentality: "Genuine film drama,"
Kracauer wrote in an early review, "has the task of rendering
ironic the phantomlike quality of our life by exaggerating its
unreality and thus to point toward true reality." This is a quint-
essentially modernist posture, of course. Korine might be a
modernist, after all, but if there's one thing that makes him the
product of a postmodern age, it's that we can't be totally sure.[40]

I think Manohla Dargis said it best in her phenomenal
New York Times review:

> At once blunt and oblique, *Spring Breakers* looks different de-
> pending on how you hold it up to the light. From one angle it
> comes across as a savage social commentary that skitters from

one idea to another—white faces, black masks, celebrity, the
American dream, the limits of self-interest, the search for an
authentic self—without stitching those ideas together. From
another it comes off as the apotheosis of the excesses it so spectacularly displays. That Mr. Korine appears to be having it both
(or many) ways may seem like a cop-out, but only if you believe
that the role of the artist is to be a didact or a scold. Mr. Korine,
on the other hand, embraces the role of court jester, the fool
whose transgressive laughter carries corrosive truth. He laughs,
you howl.[41]

Spring Breakers *looks different depending on how you hold
it up to the light.* This line is perhaps modified from the poem
"Water," by Philip Larkin, which picks up an interesting reso-
nance here:

If I were called in
To construct a religion
I should make use of water. . . .
And I should raise in the east
A glass of water
Where any-angled light
Would congregate endlessly.[42]

Dargis shines light on another point that complicates the
notion of auteur domination: as much as film can subsume
physical matter under one consciousness, it also takes conscious ideas and incarnates them in physical things. A film
takes root in one consciousness, sometimes, but it inevitably
escapes that mind and enters an interpersonal sphere. Auteurs
hold film strips up to the light of day before they hold them
up to the light of the projector for all to see. To make a film is
to raise a creative wellspring away from yourself, to *distance*
it from yourself; to let physical manifestations of truth bubble

up to the surface of their own accord; to let the light that transcends any one person shine on the product of interpersonal work. As much as filmmaking can empower the self, it also requires a relinquishing of that self, a critical passage from self into the world beyond.

When I made the *Hobos United* trailers, I think I understood this at some basic level.* It wasn't the result of a vulnerable consciousness. It played with tropes so woven into the cultural fabric that even though I knew nothing of the October Revolution and couldn't foresee that superhero movies would come into vogue, it didn't matter. It was *camp*, it was *satire*: the messianic figure prophesied by "wizards and wise ones," who ends up being different than expected; the team, named after their skills, bound together, seeking justice against the heartless products of capitalism run amuck. It's a Joseph Campbell formula, basically. And yet, if I look close enough (too close? It's always a temptation, overanalyzing texts, even my own), I can see in these films my own Sunday School-made defiance, my personal longing to revolt against power, reified, pushed away from myself, and elbowed in the ribs. It wasn't a film about me, and that was the crucial point: I could laugh at my own desires, unaware that I was skewering myself.

This was why campy, satirical film was a perfect medium. It allowed an extension of myself, an expansion of my subjectivity, and a liberating projection of my subjectivity into physical objects, into a fictional narrative, where I could hold my anger up to the light of day and begin to take myself less seriously.

---

* And when I made other films, too: like *Beauty and the Bubs*, in which my friend Aaron wore a dress and little plush ball breasts and was fought over by two stupid, douchey guys played by my friend Josh and me. Or *SIU: A Failed Operation*, a spy film in which a supposed methane gas leak at Irvine Presbyterian Church was actually caused by my youth pastor Ryan's farts. We gave Ryan the film as a Christmas gift.

＊ ＊ ＊ ＊ ＊

When did I begin to get this camp aesthetic, I wonder? By fifth grade, certainly. But Mom, with her Human Development MA, says that's not right: it's an uneven process, according to Jean Piaget, but kids develop the skill to alternate between concrete and abstract intelligence—the type of intelligence necessary for ironic appreciation—sometime between middle school and high school.

She answered this question after we saw *Joseph and the Amazing Technicolor Dreamcoat* at a large community theater in Kerrville, Texas. It was a marvelously entertaining show, all the better in a small-town performance venue. Not only is Andrew Lloyd Webber's score as giddy with stylistic appropriation as my *Hobos United* trailers, but the lunacy of the shameless appropriation—country, '6os pop, Elvis impersonation, steel drum Calypso, stuffy French accordion nonsense, all grafted into a well-worn Bible story—lent itself to the manic energy required for a small town cast to perform a full-scale Broadway production.

The small town helped smooth out some of that show's issues. *Joseph* can give off the whiff that, while Webber clearly wants to affectionately kid twentieth-century styles, he holds less affection for the story he's evoking. (A lyric from Joseph's climactic "Close Every Door": "Children of Israel/Are never alone/For we know we shall find/Our own peace of mind." Israel is merely searching for its "own peace of mind"? Give me a break.) The story feels a bit like a narrative scaffold, a simple skeleton. It's hardly better than a flannelgraph; in fact, theologically speaking, it's probably even worse. Webber and Tim Rice's work can feel like appropriation as denudation, as interiority leached—or ignored, at the very least. Warhol would be proud.

The idiosyncrasies of the all-too flesh-and-blood small-town actors breathed life into a show that can feel slick and empty. There's a bit in "Notes On Camp" when Susan Sontag writes: "Pure Camp is always naïve. Camp which knows itself to be camp is usually less satisfying. . . . When self-parody lacks ebullience but instead reveals (even sporadically) contempt for its materials . . . the results are forced and heavy handed, rarely Camp."[43] *Joseph*, professionally performed, can feel like it holds, if not contempt, borderline apathy—which may in fact be a lesser form of contempt, a lesser form of defiance—for its non-musical materials. It crops the edge of the image to keep out anything that might add depth, perspective, complication.

But in small-town Kerrville, the smooth show was layered with human texture. Cast members worked so hard, through the whole production, to make the best damn show possible, and many couldn't help but exude the beautiful limitations of the nonprofessionals they were. The lack of female cast members led one of the tallest, most handsome men to transform into a white-faced, red-lipped, pendularly boobed Vegas showgirl in Pharaoh-Elvis's palace. He took the role with ebullient zeal. Women played soft skinned, buttoned nosed, head scarfed brothers with plucky masculinity. Older men flung their limbs with torrential abandon, trying to keep time, their mouths agape. The oldest cast member, playing Jacob, wandered the stage with a frown that either spelled existential horror or tragic constipation. And the show's best performers—multi-tattooed, multi-ethnic, from all over the United States—came from Kerrville's highly-regarded drug rehabilitation facilities. (The program bios were mercifully curt: "moved to Kerrville recently" they said. No questions asked.)

I watched with wide-eyed pleasure. *Webber and Rice's deliberate camp is being out-camped*, I thought. "The pure examples of Camp," Sontag says,

> are unintentional; they're dead serious. . . . Persons can even be induced to Camp without their knowing it. Consider the way Fellini got Anita Ekberg to parody herself in *La Dolce Vita*. . . . In naïve, or pure, Camp, the essential element is a seriousness, a seriousness that fails. Of course, not all seriousness that fails can be redeemed as Camp. Only that which has the proper mix of the exaggerated, the fantastic, the passionate, and the naïve.[44]

What better way to describe the mix on the Kerrville stage?

I realize that my Sontag invocation might seem insulting to those hardworking performers. They wanted to do justice to Webber's hollowed-out picture, whatever "justice" means in this case. But it's important to understand that, for Sontag, for me, it's the *seriousness* that fails, not the production itself. The production *glistens* because of this inherent humanity: it's pure camp because there is nothing quite as pure as failed seriousness. It denies the glossiness of a limited image and the condescending attitude of defiant irony. And this quivering, energized manifestation of vulnerability can delight us if we face it head-on. Our laughter is not cruel laughter, necessarily—and even if it is cruel laughter, or uncomfortable laughter, or a-little-bit-of-both laughter, it can easily relax into the laughter of deeply felt recognition: *those people onstage are bravely displaying what I so often am*. I'm like them, just as I'm like the hobo in the trailer: standing with my pudgy chest out, brazenly facing the world head-on.

In his preface to the 1961 edition of *The Screwtape Letters*, C. S. Lewis criticizes Goethe giving Mephistopheles the capacity to laugh. "The humorous, civilized, sensible, adaptable Mephistopheles has helped to strengthen the illusion that evil is liberating," he says, but "humor involves a sense of proportion and a power to seeing yourself from the outside. Whatever else we attribute to beings who sinned through pride, we must not attribute this. . . ."[45] Satan lacks the capacity to see his own failed seriousness and laugh. He can't take joy in how we turn Webber's slick apathy into a quivering manifestation of human passion mixed with charming frailty.

To say this is to suggest that there is, in fact, a moral benefit to laughing at failed seriousness. My *Hobos United* camp was deliberate, of course. But it was exaggerated, fantastic, passionate, naïve. It gave me an opportunity to bring my subjectivity out into the world and to unintentionally scrutinize my own defiance: to see my own characteristics from the outside, to kid them. It was a crucial bridge from my fragile ego to the wacky world beyond. Stories of conversion and ego-release are often limited to large gatherings and pyrotechnic tears and moments of intense seriousness. It looks like this for many. But those of us who are attuned to and weary of sentimentality, to forms of "beauty" as trite and hollow and plastic as ceaseless cynicism, keep a wide berth from these gatherings. Far more quietly, and far more effectively, for me, were the effects of a gentle irony that helped me slowly, ever so slowly, learn to take my own image, my hard-won self, less seriously: to pour my ideas into water, to hold the water away from myself.

It was the summer before tenth grade, after our move to Texas, after my Pastor's Kid life, when I had a long conversation with my friend Ben in the heavy humidity of a Galveston June. I don't remember where we started, but I'll never forget where he went: how are we, as Christians, to proclaim that our truth is the Truth, that it is superior to other people's truths? What arrogance is that? What foolishness is that? He brought out an alternate schematic taken from his brother, who, in turn, took it had from his college's Comparative Religion class: Truth is like a swimming pool. Different religions are like different people jumping into the pool. Some cannon ball in, some dive, some spin around in the air—they all do things differently, but they're all jumping into the same pool. How can one jumper criticize another jumper?

I had no response. I couldn't counter this appealing image, because, I suddenly realized, I had almost no personal investment in the so-called truth that my life had been implicitly formed around. Christianity was typical, normal. I spent my young life bored by flannelgraphs, frustrated and defiant of my Sunday School teachers, guilted by what seemed like Christianity-as-Humanism, prepared to answer questions correctly in Sunday School—but I had no personal stake in, no defense for, Christianity itself. I knew atheists and agnostics and people of other religions, of course, but I always heard of how they were either being reached in foreign countries or coming to realizations like C. S. Lewis. The narrative was always framed by a shift from lack-of-Truth foolishness to realized Truth. I had, until that moment, never seen myself, my Christian community, from the outside, nor considered that *we* could be the ones lacking truth. Who was I to stand for our built-in superiority?

David Foster Wallace is known for this joke:

> There are these two young fish swimming along, and they happen to meet an older fish swimming the other way, who nods at them and says, "Morning, boys, how's the water?" And the two young fish swim on for a bit, and then eventually one of them looks over at the other and goes, "What the hell is water?"[46]

While talking to Ben, I realized that I had spent my whole life swimming in water that I had generally assumed—since my dad got his PhD in New Testament at Harvard, after all—to be sensible, correct. But if there's water, there must be air. And while I spent my life blithely swimming from Church service to youth group and back, here was Ben, noticing his own suffocation, struggling to the surface, longing for a breath of fresh air. The stakes were *real* for him—he felt like he was in Plato's cave, wondering whether it was even worth staying in at all.

Once you realize you're in the underwater cave, you can't unthink it. And now, suddenly, frighteningly, excitingly, the stakes were real for me, too. I realized that it all could be wrong, illusory. Maybe, just maybe, God didn't exist.

Back home, I told Mom and Dad about my conversation with Ben. Mom was sympathetic: "Ben is so smart. And I think it's just *hard* for smart people to be Christians sometimes." Dad was less sympathetic than unsurprised, and, quickly enough, willing to act. We thought we were being suffocated by what Larkin might call a "furious devout drench"? Then why don't we put the water in a glass, raise it away from us, and see where the light chooses to congregate? Dad volunteered to lead a group for Ben and me and anybody else who wanted to join—two other church friends, Brad and Matt, came along—in which we'd take our Christian presuppositions less seriously than normal. We'd read and think and speak without assuming that Christian truth is true at all, to see if Truth would make itself known. We'd ask questions, hard questions, and only expect to come out on the other side of our questions with thoughtful spurts of reasonable doubt. To risk messily mixing Wallace and Bruno's aquatic metaphors: we'd hold our group on the tenuous surface between the evangelical water we were used to and agnostic air we might like better; it would be "a place of connection, as a meeting place," a site between our doubting subjectivities and the objective existence or nonexistence of a God beyond us.

It'd be a site where we could "project affect, project mental space," a site where we'd wrestle with the Eternal Object that might not even be there.

We read pro-Christian books—*The Language of God* by Francis Collins, *Mere Christianity* by C. S. Lewis, *The Reason for God* by Tim Keller—but we examined them and tested their structural support with a rigorous skepticism. Dad mentioned The Grand Inquisitor; we *were* Grand Inquisitors. This was exciting, frightening, and liberating for us. We knew that far too many apologetic conversations are couched in presuppositions; the point is almost always persuasion rather than open, invigorating investigation. To ask rigorous questions about the existence of God, the way God might or might not be, without *a priori* assumption—that was radical.

And it definitely required abstract thinking—perhaps even more than a camp aesthetic. Satire knows the object that it's pushing at even if the push is less of a put-down than a playful poke in the ribs. Pure camp may be failed seriousness, but it's still attempted seriousness. Asking questions without presupposing serious answers? That feels vertiginous: it requires us to, as Sir Thomas Moore might say, take the trusty assurances we've held in our hands like water and open up our fingers, with the very real possibility that these assurances might fall out or evaporate or turn into something we never saw coming. Reasonable doubt, even more than satire, even more than camp, requires a willingness to relinquish the very foundation of a worldview, the very basis of an ego.

It is dangerous. There is always the possibility that someone will turn from an immature, inauthentic faith to an authentic agnosticism or atheism. And if the purpose of religious investigation is to add numbers to God's Kingdom by hook or by crook, my dad's small group was a failure. Both Matt and Ben became public agnostics early into their college careers.

My own faith is tenuous, too, more often than not. But two significant events happened during the course of our small group that changed my life in a way that I have to reckon with weekly, if not daily—in ways that, even if I were to relinquish my faith, I'd still have to reckon with. The first occurred as I was reading "Religion and the Gospel," a chapter in *The Reason for God,* sitting on my toilet. It is in the second part of the book—the part less concerned with refuting arguments against God than providing a theological account for the Christian Gospel. Religion, as Keller uses the term, relies on the notion that salvation or honor or success is earned by hard work, suffering, and good deeds. Religion "wants *honor,* for being the best of the best," as the Inquisitor in *Sacrifice* would say. All world religions rely on this sort of schematic. The Gospel, on the other hand, is the good news that Christ, by dying on the cross, did a work greater than we could ever do for ourselves. He did the good work for us, because of nothing we did, in our place.

This was a shock! It was so totally different than the pseudo-religious humanism I got out of Sunday School: *I don't have to do anything. I am not saved by good behavior, by not rebelling, by following rules.* I was loved, but this love had nothing to do with the self I could work to develop.

From that very moment on, Christ began to function as the medium between my hard-won ego and the open, surrendered self I feel made to embody. I realized then what I still have to remind myself, day after day: I can be free.

The second realization dovetails with the first. The notion of sin was always so confusing and pointless, so generally inseparable from the rules I was supposed to follow in Sunday School. And yet, as the notion of letting go of my defiant self, of accepting Christ's radical, unearned gift, began to sink in, I thought of a heuristic, so simple and striking:

sin = selfishness, righteousness = selflessness. Or, more to the point, sin is defined by a turn from selflessness to selfishness. Despite, or even because of, its simplicity, it brought biblical laws to life. Under every externally sinful act lies an unhealthy preoccupation with the self. This makes it possible to do the right things for the wrong reasons like the religious Pharisees (or, arguably, the young man in *Sacrifice*). But Christ gave his entire self for us. And if we follow Christ, we are to give up our selves for each other.

My theological understanding has shifted in some ways, thanks in part to mentors like Ang. (It's not that Christ had *less* of a self than a selfish person but that he gave of his eternally significant self; our selves are loved, our selves matter, because they're part of something larger than themselves.) The simple heuristic pulled the scales from my eyes: from formlessness came form; from chaos came order; what was once occluded in the dark, foreboding waters of evangelicalism rose to the vibrant surface. And I thought: *since opening my fingers got me to this point of beautiful, gracious revelation, why wouldn't I wish to live my life more selflessly?* I began to understand the paradox of the Christian life: to surrender the self (the comfortable, assured, egocentric, hard-earned self) is to give the new self (open, absorptive, vulnerable, surrendered) rest, peace, and maybe even, on rare occasions, joy—both in the God who gave of himself for my self's surrender and joy, and in the other selves who are so valued, too, for the ultimate end of our life together. For the throng of friends and helpers and time-givers congregating like light in the community theater.

A non-Christian would say that I bought into an image constructed by the Church. I replaced the openness of my reasonable doubt with dogmatic certainty. I could talk about how difficult faith is for me, continually, how doubts don't evaporate, how reading the Bible tends to cause more epistemological terror than divine peace in my life, how theories of the in-fallibility of Scripture wrestle with the poststructuralist deep within. But while that might humanize my faith, it can't justify it: I'll appear like an intellectual-in-the-making stubbornly, perhaps idiotically, holding onto a childish dream.

Can't doubt be just as stubborn and vain as certainty, though? I think of Wiman's quote: "Be careful. Be certain that your expressions of regret about your inability to rest in God do not have a tinge of self-satisfaction."[47] I think of what Zadie Smith told *Interview Magazine* with refreshing honesty: "[My husband] Nick always says this about me, and it's true, I have to do everything I can to not be a Christian. I have to put all my energy into not being religious. It's a daily effort."[48] Doubt is a *daily effort* with its own mental sacraments. Would I rather spend my days struggling to deny Christ for the sake of a Godless world—or a world in which God is inscrutable, at least—or struggling to believe in the beauty of a sacrificed Christ in a world that so often feels Godless?

If the answer seems obvious to me, it's because there's an-other answer: for the Christian, the notion that you've "bought into" a limited or insufficient image isn't accurate. It's not like you weighed your options and drew Pascal's wager on a cock-tail napkin and decided to hedge your bets. When I sat on my toilet, when I read about that simple, radical Gospel, it's not like I made some sort of choice: it's like an external object, *The External Object*, broke through the surface membrane of my own subjectivity. The light projected itself onto me; it shined through the glass of water I held away and it refracted straight at me. Distinctions between inside and outside, internal and external, became totally negligible. I didn't project myself into the Christian movie; the film projected itself onto me.

As this happened, my relationship to film began to change. I not only enjoyed film as something that I could make. I began to enjoy merely taking it in, too. I enjoyed opening myself up to it. And I especially enjoyed film's capacity to manifest filmmakers' willingness to ask challenging questions, to use film to open themselves up to the world beyond them. As high school ended, I discovered one filmmaker who does this particularly well: Terrence Malick. Malick loves asking difficult questions. They're often voiced by his characters, but not always. *The Thin Red Line,* the first Malick film I saw, is set in the Pacific Theater during World War II. It begins with anonymous narration: "What's this war in the heart of nature? Why does nature vie with itself? The land contend with the sea? Is there an avenging power in nature? Not one power, but two?" Questions run throughout the film, voiced by different soldiers on Guadalcanal: "This great evil, where's it come from? How'd it steal into the world? What seed, what root did it grow from? Who's doing this? Who's killing us, robbing us of life and light, mocking us with the sight of what we might've known?" "We were a family. How'd it break up and come apart, so that now we're turned against each other? Each standing in the other's light. . . . What's keepin' us from reaching out, touching the glory?"

This omniscient consciousness is clearly Malick's consciousness, a sifting, searching consciousness, asking the same sort of questions I asked with my friends every Sunday evening as we met in our sunroom's fading light. But the questioning consciousness is never answered—not verbally, at least. Malick's unanswered questions have been interpreted by some as implications that his universe is a Godless one. Perhaps that's what Matt and Ben would think: Malick's characters ask and God refuses to answer. But to do that requires one to deny what makes Malick such a stunning filmmaker: he knows that the brilliance of the cinematic medium lies in its ability to open us up, to draw us close to the beautiful objects in the world that serve as signs of the One who made them.* His temporal medium helps us spend time with these created things. In films about war and loss, he refuses to deny the beauty of natural objects: hanging vines, scaly crocodiles, striking yellow finches, bubbling magma, pouring waterfalls, towering pines, morphing clouds of black bats, striped canyon walls, desert rocks overlapping like uneven shingles, the shimmering surface of a New England pond.

It's possible to dismiss Malick's films. You can shrug them off as slick images that lie about a nonexistent Beauty underlying the very not beautiful world we live in. They're frequently compared to shampoo commercials: glossy images selling something unreal. You can deny the power of these objects in the same way that I can deny feeling struck by The Object while reading *The Reason for God.*

But if I deny the beauty and power of Malick's cinematography, I don't bravely acknowledge how images lie—I lie to myself. To chide his openness is to close myself up, to deny the "forms of materiality that touch us," to ignore how responses to our tortured questions seem to float on his surfaces in ways that are immediate, sensual, and oblique all at once. Revelations occur on Malick's surfaces. They form a meeting place between the temporal and the eternal, even if we can't articulate how or why this is so. Some filmmakers, like Harmony Korine, help me understand the subjectivity of characters unlike myself. They teach me empathy. Others, like Malick,

---

* Malick is also, interestingly enough, a scholar and translator of Martin Heidegger, who, in his later work, wrote object-oriented—or dare I say Object-oriented?—things like: "man does not have control over unconcealment itself, in which at any given time the actual shows itself or withdraws. . . . Whenever man opens his eyes and ears, unlocks his heart, and gives himself over to meditating and striving . . . he finds himself everywhere already brought into the unconcealed."[49]

hold natural water up to the light and help us voice, in spite of ourselves, the last lines voiced in *The Thin Red Line*: "Oh, my soul. Let me be in you now. Look out through my eyes. Look out at the things you made. All things shining."

Javert Likes Stars, February, 2011

CHAPTER 5

VOICE

MY FRIEND Brooks, sitting across from me at Jones Coffee in Pasadena, just laughed.

"What?"

"As you pulled out your iced coffee straw, it made the same tone as the song, right on the right beat."

Music is funny like that. It shows up in unexpected places.

✶ ✶ ✶ ✶ ✶

Go to a party and try talking to a stranger about media. It'll probably go pretty well. It'll jury-rig a bridge between the two of you, especially if you have one or two mediums that you like a lot in your back pocket—unless, of course, it won't. Sometimes, when I tell people that I study film, I see them tense up and look down at the carpet and sheepishly admit that they don't like movies very much. Our eyes then rove around the room, searching for alternative structural solutions for an *ad hoc* bridge. Entertaining isn't always easy—especially if I try to entertain sports.

For some, sports functions as a borderline-transcendent medium. It's a portal to otherwise-unimaginable interpersonal connection. On the field or court, sweating, shoving, passing, teammates connect in ways far more carnal than photography. In the bar or on the living room couch, viewers treat the flat screen like a luminescent pulpit.

In elementary school I, along with most of my peers (encouraged/forced by their go-forth-and-conquer-the-world type parents), played regional soccer. I spent my first game with my arms jammed down my bright red, elastic shorts, all the way though and out the bottom. I wandered aimlessly, far from the ball, staring at the eucalyptus trees lining the field, listlessly. With soccer (and all sports, really) I encountered the cartoon Israel problem all over again: the green, sunny regulation length fields with their geometrically rigid borderlines were too plain, identical, boring. This issue still plagues any attempt I make to watch televised sports. The *mise-en-scene* is always so disposable.*

When I look at sports I see only competition, stubborn clan-picking, emotional attachment to superfluity—factor out economics and there are no real-world *stakes* involved—and on-field aggression spreading, metastasizing, from field to bar.

---

* That said, I wouldn't argue with the claim that the silk-stockinged dandy who uses the term "*mise-en-scene*" to talk about sports is truly unworthy of them.

(Say what you will: cinephiles don't settle their disagreements with fists.) I don't see the fruitful connection, teamwork, excellence pursued. I need other people, other mediums, to explain—or, even better, *exemplify*—the good of sports in patient, detailed ways, to paint a picture that communicates their subjective passion. Films like *Moneyball, Chariots of Fire, Silver Linings Playbook,* and television shows like *Friday Night Lights* inch me ever closer to comprehending (if not internalizing, inhabiting) the "love of the game": its use as a mental exercise, as a developmental aid, as a vehicle for interpersonal connection. I start to feel out what Peter Schjeldahl (nicely cribbed by Lauren Winner in *Still: Notes on A Midfaith Crisis*) would call "what I would like about this if I liked it."[50]

But I've put much more work into understanding and trying to love another medium that rarely strikes me with visceral immediacy: music.

In a standout scene from *Love and Mercy*, the rather wonderful biopic I saw for a second time last night, a middle-aged Brian Wilson (of the Beach Boys, played with loose, squinting instability by John Cusack) sits down at a piano with Melinda Ledbetter, the radiant Cadillac saleswoman willing to give him both love and mercy. Brian, hunched over slightly, glances up briefly and then closes his eyes and tightens his lips as if about to pray. His hands suddenly hit the keys in a quick flash of warm, syncopated chords. They're major chords and then they're modulated, growing, blossoming.

"That's absolutely beautiful," Melinda whispers.

"Thanks."

"What is it?"

"Oh that's just something that I came up—when I saw you."

She blushes and exhales. "What are you going to do with it?"

"Nothing." He waves his hand. "It's gone. That was just for you." He stares into her eyes, direct and kind. The corners of his mouth turn up ever so slightly.

"That's so incredible. That . . . just, just, like, came out of you. Is that how it works?"

"Yeah. Sometimes. Sometimes your inner voice wants to express itself and every once in a while, every blue moon, your soul . . . comes out to play, you know? Can't be rushed. It's like a kid, it's just nature, but . . . yeah."

It's a lush, open moment, like the note from a quivering chime on a mountaintop. *Love and Mercy*'s most impressive, winning feat is its ability to convey how, for musicians like Wilson, music isn't a representation or a translation of conscience: it's an emanation of consciousness itself. It "just comes up." Your soul comes out to play. Atticus Ross's soundtrack—his sound*scape*, his sound collage—embodies a new type of diegetic sound; the mixture of synths and riffs and echoing, chiding voices exist in film's world, front and center, but in a place no camera can properly tread—Wilson's mind. Wilson's auditory hallucinations (products of a schizophrenia-like disorder) provide the diverse tones that build up his brilliant records. At one point, the camera even inhabits the POV of a sonic tremor from the dad-given slap that silenced one of Wilson's ears; it tunnels into his ear canal and plunges deep into his dark, broken soul.

It's all music to him. And with Ross's delicate touch, it's all music to us, too. We lie on Brian Wilson's trembling wavelength. We feel all of his vibrations: good, bad, sad. Movies like *Love and Mercy* help me tune into the sublime connection that listeners and creators feel between music and soul, soul and the wider world.

At a Pasadena alehouse my friend Courtney, an actress, laments how Christian theater is so trite, brittle, bad. But there *must* be a way to communicate the Gospel though theater somehow! It must be possible. Or not, I think: "Some mediums are just better at communicating or exemplifying certain truths and mental states than others. I'm just not sure that that sort of internal, spiritual shift is best conveyed on stage. In writing, *maybe*—"

"—or in music." Courtney responds. "Music is the only art form that is totally unimpeded."

I remember standing with another friend in a small, bearded crowd in a daycare-center-turned-music-venue so far in East Bushwick that's it's almost Queens, nodding along to a dimly lit experimental metal band (don't ask) and thinking of the remarkable similarities between our grungy group, longing to be filled by the sensory force erupting from a little wooden stage, and the crowds of worshipers that gather on Sunday mornings; I remember how Howard Belsey, the art scholar who hates figurative art in Zadie Smith's *On Beauty*, cannot even save his jaded, defiant soul from music's emotional power at a funeral:

> He was greeted . . . by a wash of music. It poured down from above, from a balcony. There eight young men . . . were lending their lungs to an ideal of the human voice larger than any of them. Howard, who had long ago given up on this idea, now found himself—in a manner both sudden and horrible— mortally affected by it. He did not even get the opportunity to check the booklet in his hand; never discovered that this was Mozart's *Ave Verum* . . . no time to remind himself that he hated Mozart. . . . The song had him. *Aaah Vay-ay, Aah, ahh, vay* sang the young men; the faint, hopeful leap of the first three notes, the declining dolour of the following three; the coffin passing so close to Howard's elbow he sensed its weight in his arms . . . he was tasting salt, watery salt, a lot of it, and feeling it in the chambers of his nose; it ran in rivulets down his neck and

pooled in the dainty triangular well at the base of his throat. It was coming from his eyes. He had the feeling there was a second, gaping mouth in the centre of his stomach and this was screaming.[51]

And I agree with Courtney, in theory. Music is like an IV straight from world to soul: nourishing, replenishing—and drawing our revitalized souls out into the world, too.

In a 2014 study, neuroscientists tried to find out why certain songs make us want to dance. They created a survey asking people to rate a variety of drum patterns and select the ones that made them want to dance the most. Some were simple rhythms with regular beats (think Drum Class 101) while others were complex, layered rhythmic patterns with lots of unexpected gaps where regular beats should go. Then there were beats that avoided both extremes, "patterns that had a sort of a balance between predictability and complexity,"[52] explained the study's leader, Maria Witek. These were the beats that made people want to get up and dance, worldwide, because "there's enough regularity to sort of perceive the underlying beat, but also enough complexity to sort of *invite* participants to synchronize to the music." As NPR's Michaeleen Doucleff puts it, "it may be more about what's missing from the song than what's there."[53] Witek elaborates: "Gaps in the rhythmic structure . . . provide us with an opportunity to physically inhabit those gaps and fill in those gaps with our own bodies." Music isn't just something we listen to. It's something we do. It's something we become. It's something we *physically inhabit*.

Perhaps a better point for comparison might be the water cycle. Music is constantly trickling in, soaking down deep and nourishing, below the surface, while it's also rising up and spreading out and leavening into broad, multidimensional clouds that please and shade and pour on us all. Music draws us to physically inhabit the world around us; it fills us up with beauty and inspires us to become beauty; it gives us beauty and inspires us to release beauty, to join into beauty, to share beauty.

Or it should. I gel with music a little more than sports; it's not that I don't "get it," exactly, but that it tends to hit my ear canal and mull around there pleasantly, innocuously, for a while, instead of traveling straight down the superhighway from ear to soul. I go to concerts and I inevitably tune out, blissed, only snapping back to full attention in moments when I remember how much money I put down to get my ears massaged. So when I see portraits of people like Brian Wilson, or mix with the ecstasy-ridden crowds at Austin City Limits, I think, jealously: *If only music could touch* me *like that.* My superhighway, if it will ever exist, is still under construction. It has been for a long time.

Many kids love to sing. I hated it. In concerts in front of the chapel at Shepherd of Peace Preschool I stood silent, stoic, feeling downright embarrassed. This was prompted both by the shout-singing little kids do—it just sounded so *bad* to me, even then—and the emotional vulnerability of the whole affair. The little public singer is the singer with a strong sense of self, a self that's willing to be both brash and vulnerable, and my will was just too timid. Children's songs were always so wonky, weird, and stupid, too. What were those hand motions all about, anyway?

And, most significantly, my nemesis loved to sing. By nemesis, I mean my younger sister. When it came to a sense of self, a strong will, an ear-to-soul connection, Kara and I were complete opposites. As a toddler, Kara loved nothing more than to stare at her wide, brown saucer eyes in the full length mirror, fascinated and even proud of her little self. Her strong will came readymade. She shout-sang with Ethel Merman-like confidence all day, every day, without the slightest hint of self-consciousness. If she had any idea how bad it sounded, she didn't care. She's learned to turn the volume down, but, even to this day, Kara wears her emotions on her sleeve and weaves them into song. Her self was formed from neither superficial image nor defiant humor: it just rose from her soul and erupted from her lips.

It was totally aggravating. Perhaps a "deep" character study would say that I was jealous of her confidence, but are introverts really jealous of extroverts? Internal processers really jealous of verbal processers? Timid, self-conscious people really jealous of those without self-awareness? I think not. I was merely annoyed by the constant noise and, more significantly, *embarrassed* by her grand freeform self that imposed itself on everyone, everywhere, with its insufferable music. By staking her clamorous claim on my eardrums she stuck a sonic claim on my own self—and I couldn't fight it.

"Shhhh. Stop *singing!*" I'd cry. But asking Kara to stop singing was like asking her to lobotomize her own mind. It was impossible. She'd get mad—"Nathan, leave me *alone!*"—and keep on piping with even more vigor. And to make it all exponentially worse, my parents rarely stepped in, because she never meant to harm me. She didn't sing to defy my wishes; she sang because she couldn't imagine living in any other way. And so I was the one who, in an effort to keep my mind pure, safe, unembarrassed, had to push against her own sense of self, to curb her strength—and for that, I most certainly *did* get in trouble. Since I couldn't use requests to get Kara to stop enervating my feeble mind-in-the-making, I figured that the only viable possibility was to make her feel as bugged and powerless as she made me feel.

This was easy, fortunately. When a heart is worn on a sleeve, it's easily enflamed. Kara told Mom and Dad that she liked a boy named Parker in her kindergarten class; Dad told me; I teased her. (She then refused to tell my parents any boy-related news until middle school). A ratty, weathered, red and white lined rag that was once Mom's nightgown—Kara's Nighty—was a Safety Object; I stole it from her; "It's my Nighty!" she cried as we pulled, tug-of-war style, from either end; it ripped in half. She cried. She created the term "stupey," an abbreviation of stupid, and decided that she was the only one who could use the phrase; I called her stupey all the time. Kara's nemesis was a boy named Tyler; I loved to talk about her "crush" on him. When we made up games to play, I created extensive rules and, as she puts it today, I "had to win." When we made videos, her creative input was utterly unwelcome. When we watched movies, I demanded the greatest quantity of microwaved popcorn. (Beth, always a clever mediator, gave us equal amounts but placed my popcorn in a larger plastic bowl.) I isolated her favorite musical videos (*Joseph and the Amazing Technicolor Dreamcoat* and a truly atrocious set of films starring a roly-poly Pied Piperish clown named Wishing Well Willie, in particular), the ones she would appropriate songs from to sing repeatedly, as sources of ceaseless mockery.

Every tease earned an instantaneous explosion: "*Nathannn*!!" And then my parents would punish me while she would keep on singing and twirling and being her little ebullient, scot-free self. (Kara puts a different spin on all of this, of course: "You hated it whenever I sang things and would never let me sing," she recently told me, as if I were actually successful in curbing her musicality. *As if.*)

On the worst days, when her strong, bubbly, unfettered, musical self was too much to handle, I'd imagine the unspeakable: I'd imagine that Kara would die, or that she'd disappear at least, and then we would live, just my parents and me, as a lovely trio in a calm, quiet, unmolested household. All of the aggravations and songs would evaporate and I'd finally feel peace. The emotional clarity of this longing concerned me a bit—*aren't I supposed to love my sister? Does this mean I don't love her? Is there something wrong with me?*—but I couldn't help it. She was the worst. If I was going to be really honest with myself . . . I didn't love her.

Although my sister-directed animosity festered and sputtered into a rolling boil around late elementary school or early Middle School, my relationship to music did begin to change. I sullenly joined the IPC Children's Choir in second grade along with the rest of my peers. There I learned that it was actually possible to swap shout-singing for *sing*-singing and that it was possible for a group of kids to croon on key. Even me: I discovered my own pure boy soprano, the one I would use to defy Mrs. Taylor in the high-windowed Sunday School classroom.

By the time third grade came around, I won a brutal competition for the lead role of Little Brother in the children's-story-turned-Christmas-musical *Why the Chimes Rang*. Poor Little Brother. People deposited their gifts for the Christ Child at a local church every Christmas Eve, but he had only one lonely penny to give. My throat was coated in thick, green mucus, as it was every December (The Month of Nathan's Head Cold) but I stood in front of the church with a green wool scarf, fingerless black gloves (poverty or whatever), and a tan beret as I cooed through my clogged throat: "A penny, a penny, it's only a penny. What good could a penny be? A penny, a penny, it's only a penny—oh will it be enough to bring?" It was my first big onstage moment. My voice was worth several pennies to me.

I only felt a tinge of abiding emotional attachment to music itself, but it was a fine tool to keep at my disposal. Vocal talent provided convenient justification for my celebrity image; with it, I actually deserved some of the stage time I got. Martin Heidegger believed that our primary relationship to things is less aesthetic than practical, equipmental. We apprehend things on the basis of their use value, first and foremost, with a "ready-to-hand" attitude, while we contemplate and introspect later. Music was certainly like this for me: its uses were more important than its pleasures, especially because musical contemplation required one of my least favorite intellectual modes: the mathematical mode.

Music became especially useful in middle school, when my keen-sandals-with-long-white-sock wearing self found itself totally at odds with the freewheeling bunch at Orange County High School of the Arts. OCHSA was advertised, like many artistic hotspots, as a haven for peculiar selves-in-the-making. *Gay, straight, bi, peculiar, original, strange: you're an artist, be yourself, be who you're born to be or choose to be or think you might wannabe! Come ready-to-hand, and use the tools before you to project toward your "for-the-sake-of-whiches"! Come swim in the vast queer ocean—the water's artsy as hell!* I, never maligned for my peculiarity in Elementary School but always an oddball out, bought the bait: I could finally not only be embraced for my peculiar self-in-the-making but live among similar selves-in-the-making. When I was accepted in sixth grade (after presenting, at my audition, part of the video I made in memory of my puppy Mandy), a bright white, seven-story Santa Ana office building waited on my horizon.

If we are to use the word "friend" in a conservative sense—sorry, OCHSAites, I know you do nothing in a conservative sense—I didn't make a single friend at Orange County High

School of the Arts. My strange self-in-the-making was neither transgressively nor defiantly strange. (As I wrote earlier,
church defiance was more of a default setting by this point—
more of a simmer than a boil. I kinda started to like church,
actually—I had actual friends there.) I was timidly, thought-
fully strange, and more conservative than Id like to admit.
I have a vivid memory of the awkward moment when the
lanky, blue eyed, überflamboyant Chris gave me a kiss on
the cheek; the first time a cross-dresser called me "sweetie."*
These people, like my sister—who wanted to go to OSCHA,
but was whisked off to Texas instead—were so brazen and
confident, so brashly sure of their glittery, rhinestoned, black
lipsticked, green eye shadowed, dog collared selves, and the
worship leader at church was just starting to take me shopping
for patterned, silkscreen, SoCal-appropriate T-shirts. I was
just starting to learn how to present any sort of image beyond
the bounds of Irvine Presbyterian Church.

Hence singing became important. I may not have embodied the self-determined artist's persona, but when it came to
actual artistry, I wasn't too shabby. Acting was a little trickier—
"Stop moving your legs so rigidly," Mr. G commanded as I
robotically paced around the front of the fourth-story classroom, performing a monologue about the inanity of *Moby
Dick*—but the mathematical rigidity, the pre-made precision
of vocal music, gave me a template to lean on, a template to

---

*An uncomfortable eighth grade moment: Mom and I
joined a large swath of delighted OCHSA students to see Chris
Columbus's *Rent*. How strange it was to be caught between the
endower of my geometrically rigid, clean-lined Irvine youth
and this (brave? terrifying? both?) new world of premarital
sex and homosexuality and bisexuality and AIDS and volatile
rock opera. To my relief and confusion, Mom liked the movie.

perform into. I could hit my marks; I could fill in the lines; I would do okay. I was admired, even respected for my ability, and made it through competitive casting calls into *How To Eat Like A Child* and *Schoolhouse Rock LIVE Jr.*, where, with a small cast learning to hit our director's choreographed marks with mathematical precision, I actually found myself liked in a social, artistic setting. I was a good cast member: calm, resolute, dedicated, responsible. "I had no idea when we started," a curly-haired girl told me at the end of one of those runs, "but you're actually cool." It was music to my ears.

Working on these shows—memorizing beat after strictly choreographed beat, mentally mapping the layout of multi-colored layers of gaff tape, knowing when to switch from my quickly fading soprano into my newly-emerging baritone (not an easy judgment for a middle school boy)—brought me closest to reveling in the sort of performative pleasures that I can only imagine must be enjoyed by competitive athletes. There was no need to love the thematic substance of the shows—both were made from a mere series of cute vignettes—nor to feel any sort of personal investment in characters. All that mattered was the skill of it, the manmade machinery of it, the interpersonality of it—not interpersonal connection, exactly, but interpersonal rigor, interpersonal reliance, at least. It began to matter less how, when I walked down OSCHA's skinny, fluorescent-lit halls wearing my green REI backpack, people I knew refused to return my smile and faux-cheery "hello" (the only bit of social outreach I could easily stomach); in everyday school life, I may not have been a good performer, a good image manufacturer. But when social, improvisatory tête-à-tête was unnecessary, when the notes and choreographed points were premade, I could do okay. I won an award at the end of eighth grade for my performance of "Seventy-Six Trombones," which I belted out with the sort of gusto that Harold Hill himself—my idol at IPC and beyond, a sublimely slimy image-generator if there ever was one—would've admired.

Vocal performance buffered me over another social hurdle: my ninth-grade move to small-town Texas. San Antonio, that caliche-cut town of scientists and doctors and bankers and businesspeople and engineers and military men, dropped many of its left-brained young beside me in the Boerne Independent School District. Many of my classmates enrolled in advanced calculus and AP Biology and AP Physics when junior year rolled around. The most popular degree-to-be in my senior class was biomedical engineering at Texas A&M.

The arts were seen as enjoyable, maybe, but superfluous. When I first moved, I found a few classmates willing to dip their toes into the zany world of artistic creativity. One was Nate, the only other wannabe-filmmaker in my grade; another was John, short and wiry, one of basically two peers willing to look me in the eye and treat the new kid on the block like a significant human being instead of some strange new species that just so happened to fly from Southern California to Small Town Texas on a misguided migration. When I wore a dumpy straw hat and a red feather boa and plucked the three or four guitar chords I knew and sang a big, broad, silly song in almost-Spanish for a video presentation, John laughed his loose, wild laugh the whole time and came up to me afterwards, genuinely impressed. (He became Kara's scene partner in theater class one year later.)

But I still found my sweet spot in choral music, the area that tempered artistic unpredictability with the sort of firm, mathematical structure that Texas could get behind. Even when my ninth grade choir performed near Six Flags Dallas and I lacked a single friend to sit by or talk to on the 10-hour back-and-forth bus ride (at Six Flags I ended up "hanging out" with Maggie and Bailey, who made a habit out of somehow "losing track of me" in-between rides), I felt okay because, even more than at OSCHA, I was a renowned performer; I was the best boy singer in that little choir.

Although Kara joined choir, she had a more two-pronged approach for social cohesion: she became well-regarded in theater class, where she worked with John, but she avoided the derogatory "theater kid" label via cross country, where she ended up finding the first genuine friend in her grade in Anne, John's younger sister.

My musical capacity also helped me with church visits. A pastor's kid, a flannelgraph prisoner, a mini-celebrity no longer, Church was no longer a system I needed to—or even could, really—rely on or defy for my sense of developing selfhood. It was both liberating and strange to realize that attending Church was no longer an obligatory requirement, an "occult adult activity, specially arranged for my benefit," as Wallace might put it. Following my baritone part in the hymnal, measure by measure, preoccupied me enough to distract from asking fundamental questions, like: *Why are we here? What's the point? What do these lyrics mean?* Church turned from a fundamental, unquestionable part of my everyday existence into something tangential, ordinary, as superfluous for me as English class was for my peers. Music is the only art form that is totally unimpeded? I have my doubts.

One can only smile Sisypheanly for so long, though, before one wonders whether the rock is really worth rolling at all. The pleasure that comes from performing well is, at some point, either grounded in or corroded by the relative pleasure and worth of the task at hand. Corrosion hit around sophomore year. As I started to make genuine friends, vocal performance became a tool that merely perpetuated its own existence, and my breathless, exuberant choir teacher could sometimes treat music less like a pure gift than a tool to be used for the choir's success. She was new to the school district, determined to build a state-renowned choir program, and Texas had a series of athletic-style hurdles for her to gallop over with brazen confidence.

There was, in the fall, the Texas Music Educator's Association All-State Choir competition (for which I once spent a long, hot week learning music at the University of Texas at San Antonio's Summer Choir Camp) and, in the spring, the UIL Solo and Ensemble contests. "Contest Season" was the stressful peak of the academic year, the point at which her teacher peers would judge our (her) worth. While quality performance was an obvious requirement for these contests, the requirements were almost entirely technical—don't treat the quarter rest like a half rest; that's a tie, sopranos; that's not *mezzo piano*, basses; you're going sharp: remember that the "a" is an "ahhh"; keep the tongue right on the front palate, right there, good—and even the most beautiful songs could feel worked like a car. It was a sport for all intents and purposes— rigid, scrupulously calculated (UIL performances were rated on a scale of 1 to 3)—and I didn't get the pleasure of sports. This atmosphere was epitomized by the only All-State Choir concert I attended. The choir was technically flawless, but in the way of a bunch of talented singers who have been practicing assigned music by themselves along with the TMEA CD *ad infinitum*, who were thrown together for intensive last-minute training. I didn't hear, like Howard Belsey, individuals "lending their lungs to an ideal of the human voice larger than any of them." They sounded like a bunch of technically accomplished solo voices layered electronically, a bunch of individuals lined up, alone together.

I probably would've dropped out of choir, talent be damned, if Mrs. Hill, our choir teacher, didn't create such a relentlessly welcoming haven out of the choir room. She was just as determined to embrace her students as she was determined to win contests. She was relentlessly chatty and relentlessly probing and relentlessly kind; she not only ran on three hours of sleep per night, as astonishing as that was, but knew all sixty-plus choir students by name within what seemed like 2.5 seconds. I spent lunch after lunch in her practice rooms—working on last-minute pre-calculus homework, making music, dancing goofy dances to prerecorded tracks from the keyboard with the friends I made through choir— friends who not only provided a social foundation for high school experience, but *genuinely loved music.*

One of these was my best friend Alex. He was extroverted and honest, a fountain of churning, open, restless emotion. Emphasis on *restless.* Alex flitted around. He started to teach me what it meant to have a contrapuntal relationship. (Literally: at more than one end-of-the-year concert we performed the Rat Pack's "Me and My Shadow," a duet made up of overlapping melodic counterpoints.) His will spun every which way like a pinball. My still-developing will seemed grounded and methodical by comparison; I grounded Alex, too, listening to his ideas and emotions and gently pulling them into the stratosphere. He, at the same time, pushed me to be more socially honest, more outgoing. And his boundless enthusiasm brought the music he loved to vivid, moving life. You couldn't help but listen to the music he loved the way he loved it. He's the one who discovered Billy Joel's "She's Got a Way" and treated its piano intro as God's gift to him alone. He's the one who played Jean Valjean in the all-school musical and cried every time he sang "Bring Him Home." He's the one who spent a $1000 choir scholarship on a speaker system for his Jetta. He'd hammer out a vocal part on the keyboard in the practice room and spin around, arms thrust in the air, and cry: "Yes!! Isn't that so *cool*!?" To be with Alex was to feel the music palpate his whole body. This could've, I suppose, been a distancing factor in our relationship—the sheer difference between our personalities and our feelings towards music—but to listen to Alex was not to be put off by his enthusiasm, but to be brought into his halo of ecstasy. He was the sort of person you'd sing with, just for fun, just to hear the harmonies vibrate and ricochet off the walls and bounce right back inside him—and, if only by extension, you.

With Alex, the origin and end of music was pure pleasure. Alex was particularly receptive to sensory pleasure (a characteristic that, by the time senior year came around, drew him further from me and deeper into drug-craving cliques). While the pleasure principle helped me tune my ears to music's pure physiological possibility, this wavelength was broadened and complicated by Mr. McKinnley.

Mr. McKinnley, with his wide, rounded jawline and prickly white beard (there's great December demand for his Santa appearance), became my vocal teacher due to the underlying hope that he'd improve my chances at joining the All State Choir. We did work on the TMEA All State music and my UIL solo music, too, but Mr. McKinnley was from the Midwest, not from Texas, and his gift to me was his ability—and, he eventually unveiled, his mission—to draw away from the technical fine-tuning so belabored by the Texas public education system to, instead, concentrate on physically communicating a song's narrative essence. The technical details—the breath support, the imaginary arrow shooting from my mouth across his dark living room, the expressive vowels—were all marshaled and fine-tuned for the sake of expressing—no, *communicating*—the narrative, the theme, the spur that birthed the song in the first place. Stopping for a quarter rest just in time? Jumping into a measure on Aaron

Copland's peculiar off-beat? Holding a tie for the full eight counts? We talked about these things, but only briefly, with the understanding that I could master them on my own with due diligence.

"Alright guy," he said, as he liked to say, at a late November lesson. "Let's work on some Christmas stuff." I expected "Oh Holy Night" or "What Child Is This?" He handed me an unfamiliar hymn. "Let's just listen to it." He turned on a CD. We listened. "Let's walk though the lyrics." The song was minor, somber, nearly a dirge, a haunted lullaby: "I wuonder as I wahndoor out uhndar the sky, how Jesus that sehvyar did cahm for to die? For puhr hahn'ry peepal like you and like I, I wuonder as I wahndoooor"—his voice evaporated into a breathy husk—"out uhndar the sky."

I began to let the lyrics marinate me. I let his modified vowel sounds rub the poetry until the holy mystery almost seemed to glisten.* How strange indeed, that Jesus came to die for poor ornery people like us; how worthy of a dirge; how appropriately suffused with this strange, covalent bond of wonder and sadness.

Mr. McKinnley repeatedly stressed the importance of singing slowly, sensitively, letting the vowels almost float. I was to really consider, really wade in the lyrics as I sang them. He told me the story of a dull Christmas concert he attended once where the students were singing "that regular Christmas stuff"—the sort of stuff that OCHSA's musical theater performers belt out with plastic precision at the Fashion Island mall every November; the sort of stuff I refused to sing at preschool concerts—until a young baritone, about my age, sang "I Wonder as I Wander" with the sort of haunted sensitivity

---

* This sounds borderline maudlin, I know—but how else to describe it?

that Mr. McKinney was leading me to reach for. "Let me tell you," he said, fixing his soft, thoughtful, world-worn eyes on me, "there wasn't a dry eye in the room."

Mr. McKinley's emphasis was never on the tears themselves, though, on emotional string-pulling through dramatic performance, on pure use value. It was about reaching deep enough into the sensibility of every song we worked on to draw out elements (who knows what they were, exactly) that transcended mere technical capacity, that perpetuated some sort of interpersonal recognition, exformation—or, perhaps more honestly, for me: to impose the sort of thematic, narrative depth I found in films, in literature, on the sort of music that might otherwise leave me dry. Eventually, only eventually, could I start to sense these themes within the music itself. Texas music programs, Mr. McKinley would eventually say, are about structure, precision, competition; his central goal was to combat that emphasis, to cultivate the sort of musical value that'd "develop lifelong singers."

I'm sad to say that I haven't been singing regularly. But while dozens of TMEA All State songs have entered and left my system along with whatever the hell *sin, cos,* and *tan* do, songs like "I Wonder as I Wander" still mill around in places deeper than I knew that music could go.

Another friend, Phil, knew how deep music could go. Phil was long-haired, lanky, breezy, ironic and emotionally reserved. But like Brian Wilson, when he hit the piano Phil exploded into spontaneous song. Multi-layered melodies rushed out of Phil as emanations of his whirring consciousness. To hear Phil work out a song was less like hearing a mechanic work on a car than seeing a painter modulate colors for the sake of evoking specific moods, times, places. Phil never wrote out sheet music for his songs; the mathematic modulation was all internal, intuitive, and subservient to his pure sensibility. Sitting with Phil as he played the piano—instead of, say, sitting with Taylor, who had even more technical versatility—was less like seeing an athlete conquer a particularly difficult task than experiencing a particular mood transmuted through the will of a relaxed master. To sit with Phil as he played was to be—even if just for a bit—drawn out of myself and into his consciousness as it stretched and expanded itself on the keyboard. Although our choir teacher encouraged him to audition for Juilliard, Phil couldn't—still doesn't—care less about winning contests or making it in the music industry. He plays for the pleasure of it, the emotional release of it, and he begun to show me, through his pure passion, what music can do between people.

This reached its zenith when he scored *Sacrifice*. We sat together in my bedroom with my dad's clunky old keyboard plugged into my laptop, feeling, searching, groping, for the film's proper frequencies. Phil was patient enough and open enough to bring me into his process as our sensibilities braided together, searching in the dark for tones that would ring our souls like a bell. I already had a firm sense of that visual, visceral, intellectual project's sensibility. With Phil's help, I could carefully, methodically expand that sensibility into the musical realm. I was worried that scoring the film would be like translating a text into a foreign language: errors and idiomatic mistranslation inevitable, complexities hollowed out or underscored too brashly. Would the score make the already-kinda-avant-garde project seem too self-consciously serious or superficially heightened? It was possible, maybe inevitable, I thought. But I didn't understand music like Phil does. Working together on that late summer afternoon, he helped me realize that scoring the film wouldn't require translation and addition: it would require isolating and drawing out the emotional substrate, the musical undercarriage, that was there already. My consciousness spawned this substrate. It was embodied by the actors. And, ultimately, Phil drew it out. He understood the product of my consciousness in a way that I simply couldn't.

To find the right score with him, through him, was to understand my own sensibility in a way that I couldn't on my own. It was to also feel the thrill that came from understanding his own process with him, understanding his mind as it reached to understand the fruit of mine. We both looked to the dull surface of that black-and-white keyboard and to *Sacrifice*, that thing between us, in order to understand each other in otherwise impossible ways. The clarity of our mutual focus, our willingness to fumble toward an end that neither of us knew beforehand, brought our differences into fruitful harmony: the sort of harmony in which the final chorus was all the greater because of its component parts.

When I premiered *Sacrifice* at the Boerne Community Theater, I claimed that scoring the film was a near-spiritual experience for Phil and me. It felt a little dippy, a little woozily mystical, saying that as I sat on that stage with Craig Childs— who, when he wasn't shooting Pastor John Watson for me, was the Karl Barth-loving Calvinist leader of an over-my-head-intellectual youth group Bible study. But in the summer of 2015, in his little room in the St. Mark's Hotel, Craig handed me a super-belated high school graduation present: three volumes of *Systematic Theology* by Paul Tillich, a not-dippy guy if there ever was a not-dippy guy, and I flip through Volume 3 until I hit a section called "*c) the media of Spiritual Presence*" followed by "(1) SACRAMENTAL ENCOUNTERS AND THE SACRAMENTS."

Tillich argues that "the term 'sacramental' . . . needs to be freed from its narrow connotations. . . . The largest sense of the term denotes everything in which the Spiritual Presence has been experienced," and "God grasps every side of the human through every medium."[54] Sacrament is even related to what was once called "magic":

> the magical element in the relation between human beings is still a reality—however it can be scientifically explained. It is an element in most human encounters . . . of the spectator with the actor, of the friend with the friend, of the beloved with the lover. As an element of the larger whole which is determined by the centered self, it expresses the multidimensional unity of life.

The multidimensional unity of life, through every medium: I rescind my first claim. It wasn't a near-spiritual experience. It was a spiritual experience.

✶ ✶ ✶ ✶ ✶

Phil was heading to music school when he got the call from his dad. We, my family, with Alex and Phil, were heading up to tour the University of Texas at Austin. I would check out their radio-television-film program; Alex and Phil would look at music performance. We would use our "college days," three days per year allocated for college visits, and skip Friday classes. It was so fun to goof off, crammed in the back seat of the Honda Odyssey with those guys. The evening felt flushed. Its eyes were on the future. Even Phil was open, comfortable; we were grooving.

His phone vibrated. "Hi. . . . *What*?! . . . No. . . . How?"

Long silences punctuated by little remarks I don't remember. Then he hung up. He was silent. I looked at him. Some sort of terse pain radiated in the silence. Then his face wrenched. He clutched his forehead.

"Is everything okay?"

"My dad just called and said that John is dead."

My mom looked up the rear view mirror. "How?"

"He doesn't know. He said he'd call when he learns more."

We sat on the freeway, silently, as Phil leaned against the back window. He brought his seat-belted body in tight, as close as he could get to a fetal position. He cried muffled sobs into his open palms. Nothing hit me then. Grievers fly, fight, or freeze, Mom says. I freeze. Kara's theater partner John was dead. My friend John was dead: it was just a fact, then.

I learned, then: Alex didn't know John well at all; Phil and John were closer than John and I were; they ran cross country together; they ran together that very morning. Phil croaked between sobs: "Pray for Anne. Pray for Anne." Oh, right, Anne—John's sister who ran cross country with Kara, who was one of Kara's few genuine friends.

We had planned to eat at Chuy's on Barton Springs Road. It's one of those dilapidated sheet-metal-shacks-turned-funky-Austin-Tex-Mex-classics. We still went there. First we prayed in the dark, gravel parking lot—for John's parents, for Anne, for everyone involved—and then we went inside and sat under the red and orange baubles and stringy Christmas tree lights. We were imbued by a zest that seemed somehow misplaced, almost mocking. I ate red chips and polychromatic salsas in spite of it all. Phil sat slumped, silent. He refused to order. He soon walked back onto the dark, graveled parking lot. He made some phone calls.

The fog settles now, but at some point Alex and I ended out there with him. He paced and kicked at the gravel in the dark. He got a couple calls as I stood by him—nothing new calls, same damn story calls—until he got the call that made him clutch at his face and pull at his skin. "Okay," he said. "Okay," he warbled. "Okay."

He hung up the phone.

"What?" I said.

"They found a note."

I remember something like kicking and punching one of the trees that stood in the gravel before I wandered back into Chuy's where the red and orange was a warm glaze, blown out by a fish eye lens, where I grabbed at my dad's arm, wordlessly, where he heeded my tug. We barely got out the back door before I burst.

"They found a note. They found a note they found a note they found a *note*."

I crumbled into his arms like my puppy Mandy and he held me and said he was so sorry and said that suicide was the very worst and I believed him and I still believe him and I'll always believe him. And I don't remember what happened next—we paid quickly, I suppose, left our uneaten burritos and carne and tamales and beans and tortillas on the table, I suppose—but I know Alex kicked at the gravel and spun around as he kept saying how it must have happened for a reason, how it *had* to have happened for a reason, of *course* it happened for a reason, and I know that Phil wrenched and said that John said to him that very morning that he wanted to go to a cross country guys' party that weekend.

And then I somehow I ended up with my arms tight around my sister in the gravel and the dark, crying. My arms wrapped around her as her arms wrapped around me, as tight as they've ever been around her, as tight as she's ever held me, as I thought—consciously or unconsciously, I don't know— about how John was my age and Anne was her age, how they mirrored us, and then my love for Kara dropped down an elevator shaft into an aquifer I had not known existed until just then. It plunged into a well deeper and broader and fuller and richer than I knew love could possibly go and I thought— consciously or unconsciously, I don't know—about the times I wished she would die and how utterly mistaken, how utterly inane, utterly *wrong* those thoughts were; how little I knew love, my own love, the love that made me; and her diaphragm told me she loved me, that she was so glad to be alive with me, for me, as it absorbed the space left by my receding diaphragm while I staggered out tear-soused breath. My diaphragm then said the same as it expanded into the space left by hers. And so they alternated, vacillated, simultaneously, reciprocally, melding into a pneumatic system like the organ of a vast, darkened cathedral pushing whimpers through windpipes, through vibrating vocal cords, saying what words will never say as we quivered together like cello strings plucked raw, beat after beat, wishing we would never end.

It was the worst night of our young lives, and we were music.

Research, ~2006

CHAPTER 6

DESIRE

WE FLIRTED, the girl and I, as we walked on trails through canyon folds in the San Bernadino Mountains, throwing the type of faux-insults middle school boys and girls throw at each other. When we returned home after winter camp, I received a MySpace message. I was new to social media in seventh grade and social media was new to us, too. For non-musicians, MySpace amounted to hardly more than a young person's hip email address.

"I think we'd work well together as a couple. Do you?" she wrote.

"Sure, I think so," I said, which meant, as it passed through her Hermeneutic Processor, that I had agreed to be her boyfriend. We were now dating. She was very excited.

I was surprised. That was so swift. I was a little excited, too, but mostly afraid of embarrassment. My family seemed to have an unspoken don't-ask-don't-tell policy when it came dating. Dating was clumsy and difficult and we glided. *Seemed* is the crucial word in that previous sentence, though: I could have talked to them about it, really, but it would've been terribly uncomfortable, embarrassing, awkward. Awkward, why? Because my self-in-the-making wanted to glide but it still felt tentative, easily embarrassed by bouts of personal vulnerability or stupidity? Probably. Or, at a deeper level: admitting to something like this would be to admit to an emotional neediness that I hadn't addressed, that I had dressed up in a put-together image through performance, satire, defiance. It would be to admit to a lack of self-sufficiency—and, most of all, to simply admit that I was dating in middle school, a move that I *knew* was a pretty stupid from the get-go. Middle schoolers were immature. I was mature. So I refused to tell my parents. I would not be a fool.

At the same time, though, if I was in it, I was in it to win it. And so my imagination compensated for social anxieties by developing an elaborate plan, an elaborate narrative, an adventure worthy of my Guys. It went straight to the ladder that traveled up the wall in the men's restroom in the Jenny Hart Building, right out the creaky metal hatch and onto the rooftop landing where boxy utilities sat like mini-skyscrapers in an urban grid. Could you see the sunset from up there as it traveled down the side of the sanctuary? Sure. Was there an hour-long dinner break between Children's Choir and the midweek Beach Club meeting? You bet there was.

So during one First Service, when I would normally read and browse the Internet in Dad's office, I took two light wood and rusty metal child-sized chairs from the high-windowed classroom that looked out onto the tennis court and I struggled to hoist them, one at a time, up the ladder and onto the roof. I then grabbed a light wooden folding table from a storage closet and took that up there, too. Mom was going to attend a baby shower back at the church that afternoon and I had to go along. I would have done anything to get out of it on a typical Sunday, but I had an idea. As people small-talked in the church library I grabbed a purple candle from a white tableclothed table and and took it up the stairs, into the bathroom, and onto the landing. I arranged the chairs on either side of the folding table and placed the purple candle right in the center with compositional precision worthy of Wes Anderson. At some point later I took a red lighter from a kitchen drawer at home and placed it in the bathroom stall behind the toilet brush. I was ready.

I sent her a MySpace message: "Meet me in the kitchen after you grab your food during Dinner Club on Wednesday. I have a surprise for you. Don't tell anyone." She was excited, of course, and met me in the kitchen right on time, of course, and we went up the stairs.

Just outside of the men's restroom, she paused: "Wait. I've already been in there." (This response still makes me chuckle, with its combination of strangeness—she's already been in the men's restroom(?!)—and naïveté—*should that really be her main objection?* Perhaps that masked the obvious sexual objection or else the practical one: who in the name of all things holy would want to eat dinner in the men's restroom?)

I turned to her, paused dramatically, and flipped my pointer finger up in the air with brilliant precision: "But have you ever been . . . up there?"

Wide-eyes, all the way up the ladder (I climbed up first, opened the creaky metal hatch, grabbed her plate, my plate, put them on the landing), all as I lit the purple candle, all as we sat watching the wash of yellow-turned-red-turned-leg-bruise-purple sunlight disappear behind the sanctuary. I don't remember our conversation, but I remember her leaning forward slightly in her tiny seat, smiling, laughing a little throaty laugh. There was ebb and flow. I was confident, conversant, the captain of our ship.

The one slight issue was the fact that the metal hatch couldn't be shut from outside. I had to leave it open and risk botching the whole secret affair, although that didn't end up being the problem: the problem was the occasional flushes followed by rising scents determined to color the ambiance brown. But much to my relief, following her lead, we quickly turned the flatulence and the feculence and the egestion or whatever into an endearing quirk of our unique venue of choice and it allowed us to laugh at the absurdity: here we were, having a lovely, romantic dinner (of mass-produced spaghetti on paper plates) while unaware men crapped below us.

Yet I, too, was about to crap on our relationship. Soon after the meal, when the sky was fully bruised and Youth Group was about to begin, before we headed through the hatch of no return like John Locke and Jack Shepherd, I added: "Oh, and one last thing. Please don't tell anybody about this. I want to keep this place a secret between you and me, okay?" What I didn't say was: "Don't tell anyone we're dating because I'm afraid of being embarrassed and emotionally vulnerable and appearing stupid." But that should have gone without saying, right? Of *course* she felt the same way, that is, until she told her entire Small Group at a sleepover on Friday night, including her leader, Christi, who was married to my Youth Pastor, Ryan, who then talked to me that Sunday to confront me about the

relationship and ask where the passage to the roof was because my girlfriend had been bringing her friends up there to
show them where we had our oh-so-romantic *scheisse*-scented
dinner and he feared that there were safety and security issues involved. Predictably embarrassed, called out, I quickly
relinquished and specified the location of the hatch and then
discovered on the subsequent Wednesday, during a bland Ash
Wednesday potluck, that the white door covering the ladder
leading up to the hatch was locked for good.

Even more significantly, frighteningly, however, Ryan
highly advised me to tell my parents about the relationship
because they were bound to find out about it anyway. This was
exactly what I didn't want to hear and but probably knew I
had to hear at some point. It was all breaking: to her friends,
to Christi, to Ryan, and, soon enough, inevitably enough, to
my parents.

After church, I volunteered to take Sandy, my one-year-old
puppy, for a walk. As we walked on the blacktop by the fresh
green grass and the line of steady, ordered, strong and mature
eucalyptus trees, I took out the little blue Nokia phone that I
mostly used to communicate with members of my OCHSA
carpool. My girlfriend and I had already texted a bit, but in
the days before large screens and full iPhone keyboards it felt
so minimal, so cumbersome, that no communication seemed
almost better than communication via text. But today, on this
dire, horrendous day, I took a plunge and called her. She didn't
pick up, thank *God*, so I told her voice mailbox how much
I enjoyed spending time with her (at a couple youth group
functions and on our one date), how fun it had been for me,
but how I had some bad news—the voicemail cut off; I called
again, continued the message with another message—I was
too busy with school shows at OCSHA to date anyone right
then, and she deserved better than that, and it wouldn't be fair

for me to try—voicemail cutoff, redialed, continued—so I was sorry if that disappointed her and she should definitely call me if she had any questions or comments and I'd love to try dating again in a couple months once my load lightened up a bit. Hung up. *Phew.* How easy and calming it was to hide behind the veil of the voicemail, to not have to bear the burden of her disappointment or feel the weight of her suffering or extend myself, my consciousness, my empathy out to grasp the ship I had just blown cannonball-sized holes in with my own hot air. I took the puppy home, sent Ryan and Christi an email explaining how the timing was bad, how I was too young, how I decided to break up with her, and I felt light and free.

Mom was very impressed that I had volunteered to take Sandy on a walk: it was very selfless of me.

On Ash Wednesday, the ashes finally began to fall on my ex-girlfriend. I received a MySpace message after the service: "You're breaking up with me???" Christi had gone to her pew to ask how she was doing post-breakup and she had no idea what Christi was talking about. So I explained about the messages she somehow missed and went on about how busy I was and how I'd love to try again in a couple months—the whole tragic, Nicholas Sparksy deal—and she was disappointed but very understanding and so we went our separate ways until a couple months later when she sent me a Myspace message asking if I had more free time and if I was ready to date again, to which I more-or-less responded, in words dressed up in politeness and festooned with a couple of "lols" or "haha"s thrown in for good measure: *naahhh.*

✳ ✳ ✳ ✳ ✳

If it took Mr. Gleeson's defiance to throw my own defiance back at me, to show me the intimate distance of my own comedy, it took far longer for the knife of that cell phone breakup to travel back into my own gut, to pierce me with not only the pain of breakup, of dissolve, of distance, but of an inability to be present for breakup itself. But in order to evoke this well I suppose I ought to evoke the disappointments that followed: the romantic prospect-less years, the many times when what I thought were romantic prospects ending up being anything but romantic prospects, the time in high school when Alex tried to set me up with several girls and received negative responses from the dozen or so he asked, the times when my sister's friends said that they'd like to marry—but, God forbid, never *date*—me, the time I went to a movie with Charisse on Valentine's Day and I held her hand and she gave me my first kiss and I said I thought we'd make a good couple and she said that she'd go out with me again but she wouldn't date me, the way it was pretty easy to make people laugh with my (occasionally defiant but mostly quirky by this point) humor, but how no type of self-determination seemed capable of giving me the relational success I so craved.

But I don't *want* to talk about this, guys. My reasoning is partly logistical: I've either forgotten or repressed the particular pings of desire and longing and imagination that flooded and left my hormonal body. Relational conflict is gripping to write about and talk about, but pure, repeated absence, pure, persistent desire? To write about that is to write about a void, an imagination activated and shut down over and over again. Living through the void, pretending that every single denial or false dream doesn't puncture another hole in the hull of the vessel of a self you've been trying so very hard to captain, is hard enough. To write about it sounds lame, maybe even petulant—to place the festering wound you wish you never had on full display. It's easier, despite the jerkish aftertaste of the whole story, to speak of the time you played with a middle school girl's heart like paddles on a violent pinball machine

("I was so young and stupid," I often say when I tell the story, with a self-serving grin like one of David Foster Wallace's hideous men) than it is to speak of the time your heart was left relatively untouched and left to rot for years on end.

What's easier? I know: to feel superior to those who treat their hearts like horny, self-determined pinballs, of course. (Yes, the pinball simile is getting away from me.) I see a recent *Vanity Fair* article by Nancy Jo Sales called "Tinder and the Dawn of the 'Dating Apocalypse'" featuring doses of reportorial anger funneled into carefully curated interview tidbits.[55]

Notice, kids, how the very problems of the media-determined culture I mentioned in Chapter 1 reappear: on the Tinder hookup app, both images ("There's a lot of girls who are just like, 'Check me out, I'm hot, I'm wearing a bikini,' says Jason, the Brooklyn photographer . . .") and sexual urges are heightened:

> even Ryan, who believes that human beings naturally gravitate toward polyamorous relationships, is troubled by the trends developing around dating apps. "It's the same pattern manifested in porn use," he says. "The appetite has always been there, but it had restricted availability; with new technologies the restrictions are being stripped away and we see people sort of going crazy with it. I think the same thing is happening with this unlimited access to sex partners. People are gorging. That's why it's not intimate. You could call it a kind of psychosexual obesity."

App profiles are scripted—"'You form your first impression based off Facebook rather than forming a connection with someone, so you're, like, forming your connection with their profile,' says Stephanie, smiling grimly at the absurdity of it."—and sex is commodified— "'It's like ordering Seamless,' says Dan, the investment banker, referring to the online food-delivery service. 'But you're ordering a person.' The comparison to online shopping seems an apt one. Dating apps are the free-market economy come to sex." But now these attributes are not forced onto us by the Culture Industry; they're created and manifest by willing users. Sales sums it up in one early sentence while describing the interactions at a FiDi bar: " 'Tinder sucks,' they say. But they don't stop swiping."

I downloaded Tinder a couple months ago at my friend Dan's graduation party in southern New Jersey. I was willing to tiptoe into the fray for this book (I sacrifice for the *art,* man), and I spent a good fifteen minutes objectifying the faces that popped up on the screen, searching through images, classifying relative attractiveness with the calculating precision of the tipsy etymologist I was. And then a tall, lanky kid with stringy brown hair named Declan came up behind me.

"Yo, you on Tinder, man?"

"Yeah, I just downloaded it, actually."

"Wow! Don't you feel *powerful*?!"

I deleted the app. I was done. I felt clean.

And so I read this article and think: *At least I don't do this! Having no romantic relationships is better than having heightened, scripted, commodified relationships. At least I'm not,* as I've heard Tim Keller describe a similar context, *dying of thirst in a big blue ocean. At least I can develop myself without sexual dependence on others.*

Jo Sales's article makes me even feel superior to social media itself, that thing that lies and exaggerates and commodifies and limits our relationships. I wonder along with her: "Can men and women ever find true intimacy in a world where communication is mediated by screens; or trust, when they know their partner has an array of other, easily accessible options?" Can those men and women, those people who are definitely not my strong, confident self? Can they, those poor souls who are definitely not me, not at all like me?

And then I get to this line: " 'Some people still catch feelings in hookup culture,' said Maddy, the Bellarmine sophomore . . . 'Sometimes you actually catch feelings and that's what sucks, because it's one person thinking one thing and the other person thinking something completely different and someone gets their feelings hurt. It could be the boy or the girl.' " And my self-satisfied life raft of a heart deflates.

★ ★ ★ ★ ★

I realize now, as a cool, dry breeze blows over the Los Angeles basin and into my bedroom window, that to write about Madeline is to write about Manhattan. When I discovered Manhattan, when visited the city and imagined living there, I felt like I had discovered the ultimate jungle, the Concrete Jungle, to grow into, to make friends in, to give myself to. I didn't just want to survive in the jungle, like I did when I was young with the help of my self-made Guys; I wanted to graft myself into a broader social sphere, to contribute to that knotty, sprawling, interpersonal organism. To give oneself to something broader: I believed that was the point of romantic relationships, too—*"for this reason a man will leave his father and mother and be united to his wife, and the two will become one flesh." So they are no longer two, but one flesh.* The ultimate point, I thought (think?) is to so eliminate the mediums that separate two people so that the final thing between them—the separation caused by that last surface, skin—is inconsequential. Giuliana Bruno writes, "The skin is a membrane that breathes, connecting outside and inside, and it defines the contours of our bodies, of our selves. So the first surface is our body and we communicate with others through touch."[56] It's not that they become one skin (an image that brings to mind Buffalo Bill from *The Silence of the Lambs*), it's that the skin itself is metaphorically ripped open just as Christ's skin was ripped open for us.

But very soon, almost immediately, I realized that my dreams of oneness with the city and oneness with another person were just that: dreams. When I met Madeline in Manhattan by the cold, brutalist towers of Hunter College during my freshman year at NYU, my delayed fancy was an aftershock of the attraction-turned-disenchantment I felt for the borough itself. Both Manhattan and Madeline promised progress and success, maturity and adulthood, new horizons and new interpersonal gratifications, and neither delivered—although we must avoid conflating the two of them since my preoccupation with Madeline was both the result of, and, ultimately, compensation for the borough that once preoccupied me before it left me lonely, stressed, and longing. Manhattan disenchanted me. I disenchanted Madeline.

On that first August afternoon after my parents, tears trickling down their faces, left in their JFK-bound taxicab, I walked alone from my West 10th Street dorm to St. Marks Place. According to *Frommer's NYC Free and Dirt Cheap*, St. Marks was a cheap eats gold mine. I don't remember if I ate but I remember the colors, the whirring data, the *pace*.

I realize that I haven't talked too much about pace. I've talked about media in terms of connection and disconnection, superficial façade and revelatory surface, but to ignore pace is to ignore the temporal dimension that shapes all of this. Perhaps that's because it seems obvious to me: our mediated world, our social media dominated world in particular, is *fast*. The connections, the cognitive pings all light up in rapid fire; it takes all of our effort just to keep up.

Manhattan was already like this, of course. The pace of social media and the pace of Manhattan are bound up together so much that they seem inseparable. When people ask me if I miss New York it seems like a kind of funny question: I don't really miss New York because I have a little box of New York sitting in my pocket all day, every day. We're all New Yorkers now, running—connecting?—at the speed of cyberspace.

So I remember, from that first day, the orange, brown, red, pick-your-favorite-color stoops with their Instagram filters pre-applied. I remember how polychromatic headshops spilled onto the sidewalk like rug stands at the Kusadasi marketplace. I remember restaurant after restaurant beckoning adventurers, packed in tight. And I, Nathan Roberts, from the suburbs of Irvine, California, and the acres of Boerne, Texas, *lived here now*. It was electric, pyrotechnic, all those big-boom-adjectives. My parents were gone. But I wasn't isolated—I was inundated. It was almost too much to handle.

It became too much to handle. That bustling marketplace became the erratic, irregular siren *whoop-whoop, whooh, whooh, WHEEEEEW*ing outside my open window in the middle of the night. It became those soaking wet walks to class, those games of Avoid The Dog Dookie Hopscotch. It became the small, compressed rooms, all those teeny damnass rooms. It became the icy winter wind and the trash that liked to soar around in little cyclones; the glass door that buckled and conceded and let little gusts into Bagel Bob's. And more than anything else, it became the horde of college freshmen too inundated by the whirr of the city to sit down, breathe, and pursue significant friendships.

It became curt, shallow, take-the-shots-and-go-home-and-pass-out relationships. The myth of intoxication is the myth of the alcoholic medium as a medium-breaker. Maybe "myth" is too strong a word, but I wonder. In high school, this was central to the arguments made by friends who partied while their wealthy parents traveled to their private islands in Belize: alcohol broke projected images, façades, social barriers, and freed the untarnished selves within. It wasn't just that Drunk Laura was goofy and giggly while everyday Laura was calm, collected, rational; Drunk Laura was closer to Authentic Laura, and Authentic Laura was what we all wanted. In a developmental stage dominated by posturing and flouting and backstabbing, drinking wasn't just fun. Teenagers fought when they were drunk, after all, but they got drunk anyway because there was an ethical imperative for doing so. It was a medium breaker.

But was it? Is it? The Alcohol Edu program I was forced to take before my freshman year told a (reportedly true) story about a group of young people who were told that they were given alcoholic beverages. The beverages were not, in fact, alcoholic, and they proceeded to act like hooligans anyway. And there was poor Janis, a pitiful punchline on my freshman floor who, the story goes, was told that he was given orange juice with vodka when he in fact given pure orange juice and who proceeded to talk about how strong the drink was and then ran into a wall at the end of our hall.* How much of this "authenticity" is an alternate image but an image all the same, or, more charitably, a personal decision to let hidden aspects of personality free themselves from everyday hiding?

I could go down an alcohol/image/authenticity/performance rabbit hole for a while because it fascinates and confuses me, but my main point is that, at the level consumed by college freshman, alcohol is hardly a medium that connects. Even when people connect sexually while they're under the influence of alcohol, their individual minds have closed in on themselves; under great pressure the aperture becomes so occluded that the whole picture blacks out. I had one so-called hookup in

---

* And then there's adult drinking, controlled drinking, which I've learned is a whole different beast: people learn (or merely exercise?) an ability to control themselves in a certain way. They slip up from time to time but they're often quick to catch themselves if they literally or figuratively stumble.

college but I can tell you relatively little about it beyond the fact that I refused to have sex (even when my mind is gone, all of my commitments don't go, apparently; another reason why I'd like to believe that my soul somehow rests beyond the vessel of a self I've built). The memory of the surfaces are not there; all I have is a gaping hole even emptier, somehow, than the absences I experienced in high school. It's an empty spot in my mind now because my mind was empty then. It makes me think that biblical passages that speak negatively about drunkenness are not puritanical decrees (in the colloquial sense of the word 'puritanical,' i.e.: anti-fun, anti-goofiness, anti-pleasure, anti-drinking) so much as they are inverse praises of conscious life, conscious activity, of a self that actively tries to graft itself onto some larger interpersonal network-thing.

And this is precisely what reliance on intoxicants cannot provide. In Zadie Smith's great essay on Manhattan, "Find Your Beach," she discusses a Dos Equis ad that sits outside of her SoHo window at NYU's Washington Square Village. It tells her to find her beach:

> It's an ad for beer, which makes you happy in the special way of all intoxicants, by reshaping reality around a sensation you alone are having. So . . . the ad means: "Go have a beer and let it make you happy." Nothing strange there. Except beer used to be sold on the dream of communal fun: have a beer with a buddy, or lots of buddies. People crowded the frame, laughing and smiling. It was a lie about alcohol—as this ad is a lie about alcohol—but it was a different kind of lie, a wide-framed lie, including other people.

> Here the focus is narrow, almost obsessive. Everything that is not absolutely necessary to your happiness has been removed from the visual horizon. The dream is not only of happiness, but of happiness conceived in perfect isolation. Find your beach in

the middle of the city. Find your beach no matter what else is happening. Do not be distracted from finding your beach. Find your beach even if—as in the case of this wall painting—it is not actually there. Create this beach inside yourself. Carry it with you wherever you go. . . . Or to put it more snappily: "You don't have to be high to live here, but it helps."[57]

We didn't quite buy this ad, at least not during that first semester: our myth (my myth, at least) was still the myth of interpersonal connection by way of reality shaped by individual experience. But what Smith ends up describing almost all Manhattanites end up living, even if we don't admit it: our lives, mediated by the city, dominated by its whirring data, its loudness, its oppressiveness, must find solace somehow; the jungle, just like the jungle of my childhood, pushes onto us. We may have initially desired to join some interpersonal thing, but we end up wanting to escape into ourselves. *You don't have to be high to live here, but it helps.*

Fortunately, the city provides intoxicants to help you deal with itself: alcohol, drugs, delicious food available 24/7 one block away from you, or, more substantially: art, culture. There are goodies everywhere you look. This is why Joan Didion aptly refers to New York as as "The Fair" in her famous farewell-to-New-York essay "Goodbye to All That." There's so much to buy there. (Notice how Jo Sales's Tinder users, with their sex-as-a-free-market-good attitude, are all New Yorkers.) And to a freshman, The Fair was fairly fun on weekend nights. But you don't find your wife or husband or your best friend at the fair.

You do go to the fair with the friends or family you already have, though, and this was a small, saving grace. My friend Monica came from Boerne to New York, too. She went to a small Christian school called The Kings College. Monica and I were used to the lulling rhythms of a Texas small town, so we knew the art of the lingering coffee date. It was our thing. Monica was an irregularity in Texas. She was a wildly successful Type A debater, a lover of Dostoevsky and Tolstoy, a pro-lifer, a wild defender of her corrective nose job and a tireless proponent of the subjunctive mood. In Manhattan, Monica was subsumed by a city that outdid her. Tired of Kings and tired by New York's tirelessness, she retreated to Texas Christian University at the beginning of her junior year.

Monica came to church with me early in that first fall, to a Redeemer Presbyterian Church service held in the Hunter College auditorium. As we parted ways afterward, she went off with her friend Madeline, a fellow Kingsian. (Madeline was not a proud Kingsian, though. Dinesh D'Souza, author of *The Roots of Obama's Rage* and *Obama's America: Unmaking the American Dream,* manned the college's helm during her tenure. Madeline was a committed liberal. She graduated from Kings, though. She just graduated early.)

I met Madeline briefly. It was a short, shy introduction. She didn't seem particularly keen to meet me.

Yet later, through Monica, through Facebook, I started to craft an exaggerated photomontage through Madeline's images. Shy sensitivity was her thing. She was a proud Southerner in the big city. When she felt too overwhelmed—she felt too overwhelmed often, it seemed—she would crumble into a fetal position under Monica's bed. A Facebook post by another one of Madeline's friends: "Madeline just ordered a root beer float online, then closed the blinds and asked to borrow the snuggie. I am concerned by this behavior." Her profile pictures were either over-exposed or drastically sepia-toned. She'd either stare at the camera with a soft, radiant smile, the smile I learned to love, or turn her eyes away from the lens in a public display of desired privacy. A selection of these anguished pictures' captions: "let me know when we're okay," "shy in the sky," "happy b-day kurt"—accompanied by a Nirvana tank top and a thick, long blonde braid dangling in front of it—"and we'll all sulk on okay," "w/e." "You can barely tell that my attitude sucks!" she proclaimed with her arms splayed at her side like a cheerleader holding pom poms at rest as she smiled a little too widely in her high waisted jean shorts as her white tank top yelled with its black, hand-written scrawl: "NEW YORK SHITTY."

Although this behavior brought to mind friends I held at a distance in high school—the friends who not only felt teenage pains but seemed to gain some sort of perverse pleasure by communally wallowing in their overblown anxiety—I refused to judge Madeline. It was hard for me to imagine that Monica, the hard-boiled put-together go-getter, would befriend an anxious, wilting flower. Although Monica was was a kind and empathetic friend, she had little tolerance for the evolutionarily ill-equipped—unless, I sometimes thought, the evolutionarily ill-equipped allowed her to revel in the feat of her own evolutionary prowess.

But I didn't think that Monica befriended Madeline for that reason. I sensed in Madeline a genuine sensitivity, a desirable sensibility, exaggerated into aestheticized camp as a form of self-preservation. This embrace of failed seriousness, I thought, was a way to both acknowledge and render socially acceptable a sweet introvert's trepidation in a cold, brutalist city. Her air quotes, I assumed, were art nouveau adornments—the building was structurally sound. The actually depressed do not flaunt their depression on the Internet; they retreat inside themselves, close themselves up. Those who actually hate New York City do not move to New York Shitty. Masochists do not feel pain in its deeper modes. It was defiance, sure, when she held onto this city that she so disliked, but it was defiance in a lesser mode.

I don't mean to suggest that Madeline's angst was some sort of hipster ruse, an inauthentic image, although the sepia and the retro clothes and the minimalist profile picture captions earn that inevitable association, perhaps.* Rather, the performative angst seemed to present an attractive emotional delicacy festooned as a shield against a difficult, image-centric city. The overblown angst enabled her to have it both ways, I determined: to buy into the aura of emotional distance by flouting her own tenderness.

I felt for her because I, too, felt the weight of the city. But I also loved nothing more than striking through air quotes, ripping through façades in order to find authentic treasures hidden behind them. (I wrote my college entrance essay about the importance of pursuing capital-T Truth, the sort of truth that seemed to hit me during my high school Dad-led small group. That was my thing. This was before I realized the significant role that irony and camp had played in my life.) So I was confident that my own desire for authenticity would charm away Madeline's façade and leave us unfestooned, vulnerable, sweet, together, sheltered from Manhattan's whirring disassociation. That's what we both wanted, right?

My attempts to punch through the façade occurred through text message, initially and consistently. This happened because I made the timid suggestion—masked as a casual question, backed by the façade of self-assurance—that we should perhaps date, right before spring break, right before I flew to Texas. ("I don't know," she answered, smiling warmly. "Maybe! I haven't thought it through. I mean, it's a possibility.

---

* After Madeline and I stopped seeing each other, Christy Wampole published her infamous *New York Times* opinion piece: "How to Live Without Irony." I thought it was brilliant and timely. Madeline didn't like it; I'm not quite sure why. She recommended a critical response published on *The Thought Catalogue.* I never read it.

Let me think about it." It wasn't a "no" and I was a quivering romantic neophyte. A not-no was a milestone.)

But text messaging made me anxious. The holes in the communication, the mysterious subtexts, were bothersome. It's not that the medium produced a false image so much as it wasn't an image at all: it was minimal text. There was such absence in the texting: the aperture was not occluded with alcohol, but the hole was so small nevertheless. At times she seemed playful and warm—Me: "Just used my fake for the first time at whole foods and it worked :o" Madeline: "Of all the places to use it for the FIRST time Nathan Robertzz."— and, at other times, intentionally distant. She and Monica nicknamed each other "Meow." She called me "meow" once or twice. So, on April 3, after we had been texting for a couple weeks, I took a risk: "Hi meow. How are you?" I texted. She responded: "Nathan! I'm good, just doing some reading for class. How're you, good sir?" I could feel her distancing re-flex vibrate through cyberspace—the systematic move from nickname to first name, from first name to formal "good sir." But I couldn't see a smile or a frown flicker at the corners of her mouth; I couldn't haptically sense her heart pump on the surface of her chest. *What did she think of me?* I did not know.

I wrote a poem called "Internet, Come Together" for my Intro to Fiction and Poetry class.

A little tap. A little routine.
Little bits of symbols and data that vaguely form something
worth fighting for.
Tossed back and forth through cyberspace
at the will of brazen thumbs and nimble hearts
Questions . . . continuing lines of inquiry.
I follow through generically but honestly.
There's a brief pause, a snap.
Its now one sided I pretend not to care

I should get this empty bottle off my desk
it just makes me want beer
instead of connection

back to work
procrastinate
facing facebook, expressionless
saving face for faces

they're getting married?
they're so young
they're my age
oh god am I old?
no
they're young
i think

a light hum, a little motion on the corner

So, how was your day?

Smile, rest into the faux leather
She's trying, sweet
Tapping back at her
Building molten melding out of artificial
electricity. Volatile.

oh god is youtube down?
dammit
internet, come on

get my shit together

✶ ✶ ✶ ✶ ✶

I have been talking to another girl this summer. Let's call
her Carly. Although the word "talking" is no longer correct

even though we still use it: we've been texting. The texting-as-relational-prerequisite is an interesting phenomenon, one that seems to both amuse and dumbfound older generations. Texting requires minimal attention; wouldn't you want to *call* someone you're interested in, to draw as close to them as possible?

This is a fine point. But I suppose, if I were to mount a defense, I'd say that if you text someone back and forth almost all day, every day, you have a capacity to reveal as much—if not more—personal information than you can through several erratic phone calls. It's more like being with someone on a road trip: you're not always talking, but you have all the time in the world to talk. You reveal, or don't reveal, as much as you want, as slowly as you want.

The ball is in your court—that is, until it isn't. Until you ask someone a question and they don't answer you back. There's a recent term coined to describe this phenomenon: Ghosting. Like a ghost, you're just a little half-present, half-absent blip in the digital void, and you can evaporate whenever you want, never respond. For those of us who care about being liked: how hard is it to hang up the phone on someone? Very hard. How easy is it to ignore a text message? You know the answer. You might be genuinely busy, after all, for all the other person knows. (From a *New York Times* article on the Ghosting phenomenon: "Anna Sale, 34, the host and managing editor of the WNYC podcast 'Death, Sex & Money,' believes that social media enables the avoidance of difficult conversations. 'As people have gotten less and less comfortable talking face to face about hard things, it's become easier to move on, let time pass and forget to tell the person you're breaking up with them,' she said."[58])

But, positively, the main purpose of pre-relational texting seems to be less about slowly revealing yourself than revealing your continued interest. It's simple subtext, almost all of it. Do I care that Carly got Kenyan pour-over coffee in Fort Worth or tea from a German coffee shop in Chicago or that she was paid $130 to perform as Belle at a princess party once or that she's grilling chicken and vegetables? Minimally. But do I care that I get that little blip on my phone that says *I care, I'm interested, I'm here thinking about you*? Absolutely. And does she care that I send the same subtext back her way? At least I hope so; I think so. Perhaps this can best be compared to the older practice of holding hands: I feel her heartbeat pulse through her hand and head my way; she feels my heartbeat aimed in her direction, too.* Back and forth, beat by beat, reciprocally, continually.

> A little tap. A little routine.
> Little bits of symbols and data that vaguely form something worth fighting for.

My in-person interactions with Madeline seemed far more direct.

She invited me to a Dr. Dog concert at Terminal Five in Hell's Kitchen on the Friday after spring break. This was a great idea: In high school, I had begun to learn how music could bond people, how the medium could bring two desperate souls into relational harmony. This concert date seemed like a logical progression. Everything seemed to head in the direction of communion: during dinner at Caffe Reggio she was light and effusive, much as she had been when I met her with Monica a few late, blurry nights. Her tenderness

---

* Isn't it interesting and appropriate that Apple has made heartbeat-sending an actual feature on their Apple Watch?

blossomed into the sort of organic warmth that I just *knew* crept behind the broadcast anguish.

Dr. Dog is a lot like the Madeline I had dinner with that night: equal parts folk and alt-rock and alt-pop, equally imaginable in both country and city, honest and vulnerable but not whiney, warm and effusive and tinged with unrequited longing. ("I walk with you everywhere I go, but it don't seem like you know. I sang your praise like an old songbird, but I don't suppose you heard," they sang that night, sweating and strutting across the stage.)

I learned about Madeline's high school boyfriends at dinner. One was a vagrant. She would wander into trash-strewn fields by the Charleston train tracks and they would drink whiskey straight from the bottle and kiss before he hoisted himself onto the moving locomotive. It was romantic. Another tried to help her save the large tree that held its old, dying branches beside her bedroom window. Before the gardeners came, the boyfriend took chains from his father's garage and strapped Madeline to the worn bark and fastened her there with a padlock. This led to a public shouting match between Madeline and her mother and her mother won, of course. The tree was lost.

I never had a serious girlfriend and I was not a Pall Mall-smoking, whiskey-drinking, country-traveling system-deploring hunk. That worried me a bit. But that was all irrational high school angst, I told myself. We are adults now, New Yorkers now. And I am here at a concert with a girl who asked me to come with her, a girl who *actually likes me for once*—a pretty, smart, sensitive girl with a bright smile, and so, during the first song, I should get over my self-conscious fears and take the plunge and hold her hand. We should join together.

We held hands and stood together, nodding along in the crowd below the wafting scent of cannabis. And yet I sensed her hold growing weaker and weaker like the failing roots of a dying tree, and, sensing an invisible cue, I let go when the song ended. I checked my phone. She crossed her arms and tucked her hands under her armpits and we spent the rest of the concert tucked in tight, bobbing along with that little, critical space between us.

Courage, friend. She asked you to come with her. Perhaps that wasn't concert etiquette; perhaps you were just supposed to listen to the music, focused, involved, dedicated. So on the way out, I tried again. She requited my grasp—but it was a limp hold, a dead hold, an excruciating, miserable hold, and I let go again.

I thought it was one of the best shows I had ever seen. Madeline thought it was pretty good. We walked to the train in near-silence. We sat apart on the A Train. We began discussing animals. Madeline loved animals: dogs, cats, rabbits.

"You know," I said, "sometimes it's kinda sad when I'm at home and my golden retriever Sandy goes into the back of the property and comes back with a dead rabbit with a broken neck just dangling from her mouth and then my parents have to figure out what in the world they're gonna *do* with it."

Her eyes widened. She physically recoiled.

"Nathan! No! Don't *talk* about that!"

"It's kind of gross, I know."

"Nathan! I . . . a rabbit is my"—she gasped—"*spirit animal.*"

"Oh, I, sorry . . . I know it's kind of a gross." I grinned sheepishly, trying to massage what I hoped was a fleeting moment of exaggerated, aestheticized hurt, but she kept sitting there, recoiling away from me. We sat in a long, empty silence. We hugged quickly before I got off at West 4th St. and I walked through the bare, early spring trees in Washington Square Park feeling chewed up like an innocent rabbit. I went to bed wishing a cliché—I wished that it were all a dream.

Madeline posted two blog posts the next morning. The first blog post is a reposted cartoon of a skinny woman with long hair and glasses. She looks like Madeline. In the first panel, the woman looks up, content, resting her chin on her fist. "Wow, I'm starting to feel really happy," she says. In the next panel, she's hitting herself over the head: "Jesus Christ what is wrong with me?!"

The second post:

> "I think I might just watch *500 Days of Summer* until all of this clicks.
> Or fails to click.
> Like a broken mouse.
>
> That's more likely."

My roommates and I fermented homemade wine in our walk-in closet over winter break and we had a "Fancy Wine Party" in my dorm room that evening and Monica came. "I love both of you and I just want you to be happy," she said as we drank "wine" out of Solo cups. "And I'm worried that Meowderline is just too *angsty* for you. For anyone, really, right now. You're a happy person. I just want you to have someone who makes you happy."

"But does she *like* me?"

"Yeah! Or, I mean," she frowned, "she thinks she does. She was really excited to go to the show with you."

"Well last night was—"

"—I know. Trust me, I know, she told me. Last night was not good. She needs to get better. We're trying to help her. Just . . . I want you to be happy."

Happiness did start to seem like a legitimate possibility, though. Madeline and I had coffee that week and she said that she was concerned that I actually liked Monica instead of her. I assured her that I didn't. (Although she probably wasn't totally assured by my assurance, she confided in me years later.) But that made sense. She then said that she would like to keep pursuing things, but, since it was so close to the end of the semester, she would like to keep things casual. Then we would reconvene in the fall and decide what to do from there. I agreed. That made sense, too. It was practical. And, most importantly, it gave us time to keep texting, to see a movie, to grab an occasional dinner. It gave her more time to call me "Meow," more time for me to call her "Meow." It gave us time to watch Steve Taylor's *Blue Like Jazz* at the AMC in Times Square. It gave me time to bring *The Muppets* to her little apartment when she had laryngitis as a light spring rain fell outside. It gave her time to enjoy the movie and kiss me on the cheek and leave me feeling accomplished and success-ful and *close*.* It allowed Manhattan's raucous indifference to dissolve in the light spring rain.

And then, on April 28, Madeline asked if I would like to attend a mid-morning church service with her on the 29th. Of course I would. She wore a bright blue dress and we sat together like protestant couples have sat for centuries. After the service, when I transferred from the 1 to the N, she said she would get off the train with me. She got off. She told me how much she enjoyed spending time with me. I told her I how much I enjoyed spending time with her, how it was really fun semester. She wished me a good summer; I wished her a

---

* The cinematic medium, with its ideas and emotions objectified, held up to the light, separated from both the filmmaker and from us, al-lowed our connection to germinate far more gently and effectively than the sweaty concert's bracing intimacy.

good summer. I'd look forward to seeing her in the fall; she'd look forward to seeing me in the fall. We smiled soft, blossoming smiles and we hugged tight. I left for the N Train, through the whirring Manhattan crowds. I felt a sense of soft, glowing satisfaction. It was a good day at the Fair.

At 3:09 PM I received a text message: "I wish we had more time to talk this morning. I really enjoyed spending time with you this semester. I don't know what your expectations are, but I do want to be honest and clear. I respect you too much Nathan to have there be any doubt about our relationship. I think you should use this summer to move on. In the fall, I would like us to be friends. I don't want you to think I have feelings that I don't."

I stared at this message for a long while. I then thought of all of my failed would-be relationships and how predictable, how banal, this turn of events really was. The normalcy was the greatest shame of all, how normal it was for me to be dumped via text by a girl who was never my girlfriend, a girl I had just seen, a girl who looked into my eyes as if she were genuinely glad to be with me.

I responded: "Okay. Thank you for being so straightforward. The process of letting go is actually something I've been working on all semester, so this is proper. And if there's one thing I'm good at, it's being a friend. Thanks again for telling me."

I went down to the bodega by Broadway and 10th Street and bought a bottle of cheap Chardonnay. *Find your beach in the middle of the city. Find your beach no matter what else is happening. Do not be distracted from finding your beach. Find your beach even if . . . it is not actually there. Create this beach inside yourself.*

The beach couldn't be found. I drank the whole bottle but I didn't feel drunk. I then wrote a poem for Madeline, a sequel to my earlier poem, called "Internet, Came Apart."

Can't catch a signal down here.

Her visage faded into the singular image
of a sand-colored church bulletin resting
on a blue dress hiding sweet white legs.
A bright-blue dress.
It was too cold to wear a dress
but she wore one anyway.

She didn't tell me in that sweet blue dress
but used her lazy thumbs and hardened heart to send
a sprawling piece of text
which drifted idly and casually
through the same breeze that
births silly sentences and drunken nonsense.

Try to remember what she looked like
but the data won't whisper. Perhaps that's the way it should be.
Perhaps the mind is like a sieve that reflexively
sighs out the baggage it don't need to carry
because it's too damn heavy.

I stand in the desert near a broken down Ford with nothing
but a pile of text a mile long,
the hollow remnant of something that seemed
worth fighting for.
It's hard to carry, this messy Ford.

Wait. I see her now.

She's next to me on The One Train,
avoiding my eyes, looking off into a well
of emptiness, her brown eyes as round as her dress is blue
but twice as sad.
She's searching the void, alone together
wish the essence of nothing could fill the abyss

and nudge away the bright blue lack.

A couple weeks after I peed out the cheap Chardonnay, after Madeline showed me how cheap our "relationship" actually was, Monica told me that it was her idea that Madeline should invite me to church and break the news to me afterwards. Monica also said that she was the one who wrote out the text I received that afternoon as Madeline rested in a fetal position under Monica's bed, paralyzed.

Madeline couldn't muster up the courage to tell me in person and I couldn't muster up the courage to send Madeline the poem.

But I forgave her that summer. Or so I said. Or so I tried. I flipped on the Forgiveness Switch. I tried to let her go. I wanted to let her go.

During the fall after my freshman year, I attended a healing prayer meeting hosted by InterVarsity Multi-Ethnic Christian Fellowship. I was InterVarsity's large group coordinator. Many of the prayer leaders were holdovers from the prophetic prayer nights we also hosted. Charismatic Christianity made me feel both nervous and uncomfortable since it seemed to quite possibly be the Christian equivalent to fortune telling and sorcery and mediums in Lower East Side shops and, therefore, insanity, stupidity, embarrassment. But I quickly discovered that the many of the "prophetically gifted"—at least the ones known and vetted by my friend Trevor, our staff worker—exhibit anything but the brash egomania that one would expect out of self-proclaimed mediums. Quite the opposite, in fact: they displayed an unnerving and downright beautiful openness to the God who transcends their own cognition, our mass cognition. They were oh-so-willing to let their hard-won selves go.

This was very appealing. It was a logical extension of what was so appealing about Christianity to me in the first place. It could be a crock of crap, but who was I to decide? Who was I to trap the power of God in the limiting cage of my oh-so-knowing Secular Age cynicism? And even more practical was what we always said at the beginning of these events: even if you don't believe it, how will it hurt you? Test what is said on Scripture, meditate on it, decide for yourself. (What I didn't say but what I thought when I said this stuff: this isn't brainwashing; your agency is not devalued here; it is crucial here.)

I wouldn't participate in the Healing Prayer, I decided. People had much more pressing wounds: I was not abandoned by my father or mother; I had not dealt with a major death; I was incontrovertibly privileged. I struggled with the city, sure, but I was happy-ish—really, I was, I promise. But then, as the predictably soft acoustic guitar music played and the prayer ministers sat around the edges of the softly-lit room in the Global Center for Academic and Spiritual Life, I felt suddenly called out of myself, in spite of myself, pulled toward a bald man with thin eyebrows and soft blue eyes. ("When I saw you, I felt that you needed prayer," he confided to me later.)

What did I need prayer for? I don't remember exactly what I said because I was so carefully vague. I struggled to find something to say that was both general enough to avoid any embarrassment, in order to keep my self afloat, and specific enough to seem realistic: I had some romantic trouble with a girl recently . . . in which I wasn't treated very well . . . in which I was hurt? Yeah, that's it. Yeah. He peered at me with his eyebrows slightly furrowed as if he knew that I was just holding out the tip of my iceberg. But he didn't say anything. He put his arms on my shoulders and prayed silently.

Then he stopped and looked up almost sheepishly, but respectfully, gingerly, and said in a soft, even voice: "So I get the feeling that you've been through a lot of rejection."

Ugh. "Well . . . yah. My whole life. Since eighth grade."

He prayed again. He saw an image this time: I look into a window that quickly turns into a computer screen. As with most prophetic poetry, this Rubik's Cube of an image can be spun in several different ways: the window is a precursor to presence* substituted by a new medium, the digital screen, that replaces the warmth of the sun and the promise of presence with an endless chasm, or else: the classical film theory interpretation and the concrete, Conservative Christian interpretation which might, curiously, agree: as in *Rear Window* and many other films, the window and the screen are equated as conduits for voyeurism, references to the masturbatory tendencies I have begrudgingly sanctioned ever since that sad, wrenching, painfully ecstatic ninth-grade afternoon when first sat on the toilet in the little rent house bathroom with the wallpaper spotted with cartoon spurs and Texas flags and stared down at the full-page spread of Carrie Underwood's retouched face in my sister's *Seventeen* magazine, trying to cope with the teasing lust that I would, right then and there, begin to endlessly perpetuate as I'd use lying images to unsuccessfully lie to myself. But as it sometimes seems to be with God, while the image itself can be held up to the any-angled light, the import of the image, right then and there, was simple, pure, and deep, like the low note from a lone chime: I tend to live my life as if I'm viewing it through a window, through a screen, from an aesthetic distance that's as safe as it is lonely. I assume that beyond a low level of intimacy, the difficult and joyous mix of romantic life, a life of deep interpersonal connection, *can't* be for me.

---

* In his poem "High Windows," Larkin refers to the "sun-comprehending glass," in which Christian Wiman finds a reference to Genesis, to "the Lord's face moving on the face of the deep, glass that could comprehend the sun, some sheer clarity of existence that both saves and rives you."[59]

And then I told the minister about high school, about Madeline, how we ended. And when he asked the crucial question—"How does this make you feel?"—I answered with a sentence I had never said before, a sentence that made me feel so stupid because I knew it wasn't true but a sentence that also made me feel like a fresh wound ripped raw from a giant crushing band-aid, a wound breathing the free air for the first time: "It makes me feel like I don't matter." Like Howard Belsey isolated from the unified choir above him, I tasted salt, watery salt, a lot of it, from my eyes, in the chambers of my nose. Salt water poured through the holes in the hull of the self I thought I could navigate—and I let it sink. The Prayer Minister then proclaimed God's condition-less, criteria-less, unwavering, unceasing love over me, a love stronger and fuller and deeper and more consistent than the love that any individual person could provide, a love that can fill me and nourish me and I laughed as he proclaimed that treasures wait for me in Heaven—*treasures in Heaven for stupid selfish dumbass* me? *How stupid* is *this grace?*—before we hugged and I left and I breathed.

A rational materialist would claim that I experienced a type of classical catharsis. A Christian would claim that I experienced healing by the Holy Spirit. In some sense, the question of the source is less important than the ultimate result, but, to answer your question: I believe I experienced both. I believe that the emotional and the spiritual were bound (and released) by the medium of the physical. And I believe that at some fundamental, elemental level, despite my undulating, ever-wavering heart, I am still free.

The most recent conversation I had with Madeline, my genuine friend, just before the three-year anniversary of the breakup of the relationship that never was:

We met in Manhattan, by Union Square, on a Monday afternoon. She wore a knitted black-and-white parka over a black
button-up with cartoon "POW!"s printed all over in blocky
script. She smiled a truly unsad smile and gave me a light,
one-armed hug and touched my arm with ginger fingertips.

She had been out of the city for eight months, traveling.
And now I was leaving, too, leaving for Boston. We talked
over a round of beers on a Third Avenue patio—about the
countries she visited, the friends she made, the time Alanis
Morissette picked her up as she hitchhiked in Canada. We
talked about her parents, how they were okay, themselves,
living their lives, sad. And we talked about writing.

"I just don't have one of those people I *know* I can trust
to edit my work right, like, a trusty, regular editor who gets
my stuff." I said.

"Yeah, Lauren was kind of like that for a while for
me, but—"

"—her style is just different than yours."

"Yeah, different."

"I mean the trick is that you need someone who can bring
out *your* best work."

"Who won't just try to make you like them."

"Right. Who will bring out the best in you for what you're
doing. They have to tell you when what you think is really
good isn't that good and at the same time encourage you to
bring out certain really good aspects of your work that you
just haven't thought about or noticed yet . . . to bring yourself
out of yourself, if that makes any sense I have no idea if it does.
And that's such a tricky dynamic to get."

"Like someone who's not trying to make you like them
and who's investing in you while also challenging you."

"I mean David Foster Wallace had that with Mary Karr,
but he was also in love with her—"

"—so that obviously helps."

"Yeah, that helps. I just feel like it happens organically. You can't force it."

"Oh yeah totally."

"It's like when you see some people who are just in a really good relationship and you wonder how in the world they *got* that—"

"—yeah, you're right, it's *exactly* like that."

We paused and looked down at our empty glasses. She didn't ask me to edit her writing and I didn't ask her to edit my writing and I glanced away from her, into the fading sunlight, and I realized that neither of us knew what we were really talking about until it was too late.

Creek By Mammoth Lakes, California, August, 2010. Taken by author.

SACRED CONNECTION

It might have something to do with the term "ghosting," or with the unaddressed post-it note on the wall by my writing desk that says "snapchat—exercise in ephemerality?," but I've been thinking a lot about gifts and about presence and absence, too, and how that's what we really want to talk about when we talk about media.

I think about presence and absence as I drive up Highway 395 toward Mammoth Lakes in the worst drought California has ever seen. Half of a once-full water bottle, severed at the waist, sits full of thick black tar dip on a curb by a sun-fried Chevron station. Smoke from an unseen fire colors the desert creamy like a bad Instagram filter. A wooden sign with burned-out letters on the left side of the road beckons: "Ghost Town—Free!"

When I think about how mediums shape life experiences, I find that I spend most of my time thinking in terms of presence and absence, unification and separation—and how the mediums are just conduits for these states. Once I start thinking like this it's then tempting to suggest that, since presence and unification are clearly good and since absence and separation are clearly bad, mediums that unify are better than the mediums that separate. Then I can establish a little hierarchy of mediums, a little heuristic, and feel good about myself.

But I don't always think like this. An article written by an old boss gave me pause the other day. When I worked for him, he was the strongest advocate I knew for the power of digitally mediated relationships. Then, most recently, as a way to announce a major foreshortening of the website we worked on together, he published an article titled "Digital Relationships Just Aren't as Powerful as Flesh and Blood."

The piece wasn't designed to discredit digital relationships, but to espouse a hierarchy. And maybe it's a good hierarchy. Perhaps flesh-and-blood relationships—where only mediating sur*faces* stand between us—are more powerful relationships. But isn't it easy to take a little leap from determining what's more powerful to determining what's always necessarily better? Are in-person relationships—so often made of false images and evasions and histrionics and manufactured apathy—*necessarily* better than digitally mediated relationships? My old boss writes: "Wherever you are, be there. This is the purpose of human beings. Love your neighbors by being present with them. Virtual presence matters as a catalyst to physical presence."[60] And so we're left with these two modes of presence: virtual presence, which matters . . . but only as a catalyst to physical presence, where treasures really lie.* Physical presence is greater presence.

Is this always the case? I'm not sure as I hike in the eastern Sierra Nevada Mountains outside of Mammoth Lakes. The colors are harsher, simpler than Yosemite or Kings Canyon or the western Sierra in general. They're not as desolate as Flannelgraph Israel because the saturation's still there—azure blue lakes and dark pine greens are wired together by clear streams running over rich brown soil—but the swaths of color are similarly striking, like a Mondrian. The peaks are steeper in the east than in the west. They're touched by the dry breeze that rises off Death Valley. Noses bleed and lips chap and fires burn. Tioga Pass is closed due to fire, we learn. We hike up north, in Lundy Canyon near Lee Vining, to avoid the smoke. The canyon is wide open, clear. Gurgling granite waterfalls run all the way down.

One day later, a nearby fire closes Lundy Canyon. "Avoid Lee Vining," the advisories say. Perhaps we should hike in the south, out of Rock Creek? Nope—there's another fire down there, too.

To hike in the Mammoth is to be inundated by a beauty so striking, so physically present, with knowledge that the beauty might fold up in flames at any minute. If that knowledge doesn't make the beauty better, per se, it does give it a striking sheen: when beauty is both undeniably present and undeniably tenuous, the beauty can be appreciated as the gift that it is.

---

* I'm not exactly sure what "virtual presence" is to anyone who's not a robot, but, anyway, let's assume that he means being physically present in a space while being connected to another physical person through a digital medium. Still, even the term "virtual presence" draws some sort of line in the sand, lessening the physical, embodied quality of the digitally mediated experience.

This isn't to say it isn't often maddening, sometimes heart wrenching, to hold presence and absence together in seemingly ceaseless cognitive dissonance. A couple Sundays before we head up to the beautiful mountains that burn, we learn that Sandy, now an extraordinarily healthy eleven-year-old, has a ravenous sort of cancer originating in the spleen, common to Goldens. With Kara in Boston until Thursday night, we decide to give her one last week.

After hearing the news I come home to greet her as she lies on the cold stone, panting softly, her stomach round, globe-like, distended. I'm both floored by the gift of her presence and torn up by the knowledge of her inevitable absence—how, in less than a week, this sweet, soft body will go up in flames.

It's a long, hard, sad, good, tiring week. I bring her cold water when she can't get up; I cook her bratwurst; after the bratwurst she then has a burst of energy and I take her on one last little walk up and down the block; I rub her soft ears and hear her familiar grunts—so very soft now, but grunts, still—of pleasure; she lays her head against my knee; I lay on the cold stone and feel her wet, labored breath against the crook of my arm. My mind does the splits: I'm so glad to be with her, so intent upon internalizing the texture of her velvet ears, the smell of her coat, the look of her round black eyes, while it's also continually, purposely, mournfully drawn to the emergency vet clinic across from In-N-Out Burger and its presence-ending syringes. I feel the weight of her absence while she still lives. I'm in the present and the future, in presence and absence, all at once. But how *strange* it is, feeling such communion and divorce at the exact same time.

This finds an uncanny echo in my time with Carly. Carly, the one I spent months texting back and forth with, sending out heartbeat-type texts: we overlap in Los Angeles for about a month. When I walk out onto Locust Street and see her for the first time in many months I feel a flash of excitement and anxiety, the flash I've come to associate with the fear and rush of physical presence after months of pleasant partial-ness. We text so easily, so pleasantly—will "flesh and blood" screw it up?

It does not screw it up. We attend a performance of *The Screwtape Letters* at UC Irvine. I meet her sister and brother-in-law. I introduce her to some good coffee; we drink good beer at Congregation Ale House. She meets my parents. She visits our new house. We go to a crappy (turned hipster vin-tage in our eyes) old diner called Conrad's and get pie and cocktails and love the silliness of it. We use a gift card to watch *Ricki and The Flash* in a fancy theater that looks more like the One Oak nightclub, where the plush seats recline and where they have liquid-nitrogen-modified prickly pear margaritas and free popcorn; we laugh at how out of place we feel. I meet her two-year-old niece, Jane. We go to the beach with our books and just end up talking instead of reading. (We've brought our books to many of these outings, and we've always ended up talking instead of reading.) I hide in her shadow so my pale skin doesn't fry.

But there is a timer on this relationship, too: she is mov-ing to Chicago at the end of the summer and I am moving to Boston and of course neither of us want to be in long-distance relationships, because flesh and blood are more powerful, and so of course I don't say anything about how smart and goofy and strong and sweet and pretty and level-headed and even-keeled I think she is. Of course I don't hug her too long or try to kiss her or do anything that would increase our flesh-and-blood presence because my mind is continually, purposely, mournfully drawn to our inevitable parting. I feel the weight of her absence while she's still with me—especially when she's with me. We sit on a towel, on a rock, below a couple who are making out and taking selfies in a regular rhythm, and we watch the burnt orange sunset over the Pacific. My right leg barely touches her leg and she shivers and says she's cold and I think how I'd like to put my arm around her back like you're supposed to do and then I think of what a bad idea that is and then, even more pressing, I think of what an *absurd* scenario I've found myself in, this crazy simulacrum of a romantic relationship in which presence and absence rub together like two sticks that want to set my mind on fire.

I feel like I'm dying of thirst right next to the largest body of water in the world. But I'm okay—she will be gone; I'll move on to a new place, new experiences. This is all for the best. This is wise. Our time together was a temporary gift.

Presence and absence are intertwined in all of our mediated experiences. The more you learn to look for them, the more you find them. They're presence and absence when the singer at the free concert Carly and I go to in MacArthur Park takes up an iPhone from the crowd so she can spin around and film herself singing—an extraordinary record of presence for the recipient of the video, at the expense of the larger audience. There's presence and absence even before the Fall when Adam and Eve are united and God leaves the Garden. There's presence and absence when, a couple weeks after Sandy dies across from In-N-Out, after I've moved to Boston, my parents send me of pictures of their new puppy, Luna—a Golden so classically gorgeous she could be mistaken for a stuffed animal—licking their faces, on a towel on Mom's lap in the minivan, running around our backyard. I wish I could be with them, with Luna, but sweet beauty still radiates from the pictures; I'm not tortured by absence in a dog's presence this time; I'm away from a dog and I'm filled by these marks of presence, love.

I say all of this because while writing this book, it has been tempting, and often even right, to climax and conclude with moments of incredible absence or incredible presence: when I'm utterly turned off by the stand-up comedy at Revision; when my sister and I meld into a musical instrument. But Revision was hard because I sensed a *longing* for presence. I melded with my sister in the gaping, airless hole of John's absence. And as I realized in Mammoth, with Sandy, with Carly, to live at all is to live in the clutches of both presence and absence. This is not a new or particularly profound realization, I know (a baby is born and then it cries out for what it lacks). But it does dismantle any hierarchies that we attempt to make, any assumptions that extreme presence and extreme absence are merely characteristics of new media and digital culture. In fact, perhaps the *advantage* of digital media, of texts and tweets and beautiful, lifelike photographs, is that it forces us to face the presence and absence beneath all aspects of our lives.

Heidegger used the term "Dasein" to describe what we'd normally call a "person" or "people." Dasein literally means "being-there," which implies that the fundamental condition of existence is physical presence. This is sensible. But this claim is, if not totally contested, certainly complicated by the media theorist Friedrich Kittler when he writes:

> In 1927 the young Heidegger called for . . . proving that actual presence was not the most noble ontologic attribute. Quite the contrary, beings such as ourselves are distinguished from others by the twofold absence of future and past. Distance proves to be a prominent feature of our being-in-the-world.[61]

Distance proves to be a prominent feature of our being-in-the-world. Dasein means "being-there," sure. But, he wondered. I wonder.

I wonder as I lie in bed at three in the morning a couple days after Carly left. I assumed that I would move on, both literally and figuratively, but my brain is stuck on what was and what seemed like maybe could've been, and what maybe, if only in a dream space, could still be. All of the things I like about her come into sharper focus, perhaps exaggerated focus, and I seriously consider the possibility that I messed up or missed out. I think of the phrase "absence makes the heart grow fonder" and I decide that I don't like it. It makes absence seem as if it's some sort of steroid shot to the coronary artery, some perverse Viagra pill. It *makes* the heart grow. I discover that what absence can do (not what absence necessarily does, since it can clearly calcify and embitter and just torture the soul, too) is clarify priorities, brighten possibilities, saturate longings. This is vital.

And then I wonder, almost as an afterthought, what this realization might have to do with the God who so often feels absent, so separated from our lives by the vast, seemingly endless medium of time and space.

And then I realize what I must do: I must tell Carly how I feel, how I treasure and value her more than I knew. I must not let the weight of absence calcify. I must not push our relationship aside as a silly simulacrum, as an image of relational bliss covering an empty chasm. I must not defy my feelings by clinging to them and turning against them through a refusal to act. I must not treat my life as if I'm viewing it through a window, through a screen, from an aesthetic distance that's as safe as it is lonely. I must carefully step into the messy orchestra of interpersonal life—not into the First Chair seat, perhaps, but somewhere where the rhythms of my soul will expand out of myself. I must find a medium proper for this project: do I draw a picture? Do I write a letter? Do I fly to Chicago?

My quivering tone may not be met with harmonious response, of course. She may not feel the same way. She may find the weight of absence too heavy to carry. She may feel something I haven't foreseen. This is the risk: I cannot demand the sort of closeness I craved from Madeline. It is not fair, nor right, to demand that. So I might look foolish, hopeless, silly. All I can do is give my tentative, fragmented self—not a carefully crafted bulwark against the storms of life but a broken, haphazard raft buoyed by the churning waters of a violently cradling grace—and reach a tender tendril out into the void. This is a risk worth taking.

I realize that this may seem like a rather anticlimactic note on which to end a book. *Big deal: he's gonna tell a girl he has a crush on her. Give me a break.* I wouldn't argue with that criticism.

Except: in a world chock full of so many mediums, of tiny texts and tweets and pics and vids and Snapchats piled miles high, is it not precisely these banal gestures, these little moves of our selves out of ourselves, that make up the skyscrapers of communal existence? Do these not matter as much as the individual stones of a grand cathedral? We must contemplate the bane of falsified images, the dangers of distance, the weight of absence, just as master builders must contemplate the difficulties of gravity and the steady, natural weathering of inclement weather.

But we must build. For we must congregate, and we must worship.

How to end a memoir in an age when Facebook wants to write our memoirs for us?

Prostrate your weak-kneed self on the shag carpet before the electric hearth and feel warmth radiate from the cathode rays, the sockets, the batteries, the LED screens. Pour your muddled, murky self into a glass and let the light lick it clean.

Reach a trembling hand into the void and hold tight to the things between us, which are, after all, linked to us all along.

Work on the gift. Knit your story into our story, stitch by stitch, bit by bit, tap by tap, and vaguely form something worth fighting for.

ACKNOWLEDGEMENTS

I offer Hendrickson Publishers my sincerest gratitude, for placing faith in a way-too-young-to-be-trusted writer and for fostering my peculiar, particular voice, straight down the line. Special thanks to Carl Nellis, my editor-turned-mentor-turned-friend, for making this process by turns riveting, challenging, exciting, and significant. I look back at the past year and a half with utter fondness; that's largely your fault.

I owe so much to my beta readers—Steve Norris and Henry Greenberg—and to my second-generation readers: Beth Pinney, Linda Roberts, and Mark Roberts. This book is the way it is because of the gracious time you spent reading, thinking, and critiquing. Thanks, as well, to the Harvard GSAS Christian Community for engaging with and critiquing my introduction.

If my prose is halfway decent, that's due to the many, many mentors who've helped whip this right-brained doofus into shape: Lenora Bryant, Sheryl Rosebrough, Lynne Halley, Penny Knox, Kathy Calkins, Beth Pinney, Michael Mah, Zadie Smith, Marcus Goodyear, Alex Halberstadt, and Clifford Thompson—for whom parts of this book were written in alternate guises.

Go back in time and ask ten-year-old-me if he'll write a theology-inflected book. He'll probably laugh. I owe my fledgling faith to those willing to approach both Christianity and myself with thoughtful, candid openness: Emmett and Michelle Raitt, Lisa Guest, Gary Wolensky, Steve Thames,

Ryan and Christi Nielsen, Mark Giglio, Janel Clemmons, Josh "Wolf" Sullivan, Steven "Apache" Lentz, Andrew "Spice" Pride, Craig Childs, Angela Aadahl, Trevor Agatsuma, and Pete Williamson, in particular.

I offer nothing but my sincerest gratitude and affection toward the congregation of Irvine Presbyterian Church, 1992 to 2007. You loved me, my family, and my peers with the sort of intention, good humor, intelligence, and grace that I so often neglected to appreciate or reciprocate. All commentary on Sunday School culture is by no means a critique of your stalwart commitment.

Finally and most generally—but perhaps most significantly—I owe this book to the unbelievable number of people who've helped nudge me and tease me and mold me into the art-loving writer-thinker-whatever person I am today. You know who you are and I know who you are. You knit me into the gift. *Thank you.*

SOURCES

1. Arthur Laurents, Gypsy Rose Lee, and Stephen Sondheim, *Gypsy: A Musical: Suggested by the Memoirs of Gypsy Rose Lee* (New York: Theater Communications Group, 1994), 20.

2. Michael Chabon, "Trickster in a Suit of Lights: Thoughts on the Modern Short Story," in *Reading and Writing Along the Borderlands: Maps and Legends* (San Francisco: McSweeney's, 2009). I read it in a *Los Angeles Times* excerpt, under the title "The Pleasure Principle." It can be found here: http://articles.latimes.com/2008/apr/27/books/bk-chabon27.

3. Dietrich Bonhoeffer, *Life Together: The Classic Exploration of Faith in Community* (New York: HarperOne, 2009), 101.

4. "medium, n. and adj." *OED Online*. Oxford University Press. http://www.oed.com/view/Entry/115772

5. Brainyquote, s.v. "media," http://www.brainyquote.com/quotes/keywords/media.html.

6. Zadie Smith, "Speaking in Tongues," *Changing My Mind: Occasional Essays* (New York: Penguin Books, 2010), 135.

7. Phillip Lopate, "Anticipation of *La Notte*: The 'Heroic' Age of Moviegoing," *Against Joie de Vivre: Personal Essays* (Lincoln, NE: Bison Books, 2008), 119–20.

8. Guy Debord, *The Society of the Spectacle*, trans. Donald Nicholson-Smith (New York: Zone Books, 1995), 12.

9. Quoted in James K. A. Smith, *Jacques Derrida: Live Theory* (New York: Bloomsbury Academic, 2005), 83.

10. "About the Book," *The Singularity Is Near*. Ray Kurzweil, http://www.singularity.com/aboutthebook.html.

11. Mark Strand, "On Edward Hopper," *The New York Review of Books*, June 25, 2015, http://www.nybooks.com/articles/2015/06/25/edward-hopper/.

12. Susan Sontag, "On Style," *Against Interpretation: And Other Essays* (New York: Picador 2001), 30–31.

13. David Foster Wallace, *Infinite Jest* (New York: Back Bay Books, 2006), 143.

14. Joshua Rothman, "A New Theory of Distraction," *The New Yorker*, June 16, 2015, http://www.newyorker.com/culture/cultural-comment/a-new-theory-of-distraction.

15. Ben Davis, "Hipster Aesthetics," *9.5 Theses on Art and Class* (Chicago, IL: Haymarket Books, 2013), 119.

16. Plato, "Republic," *The Bloomsbury Anthology of Aesthetics*, ed. Joseph J. Tanke and Colin McQuillan (New York: Bloomsbury Academic, 2012), 28. In the same volume, see Walter Benjamin's "Work of Art in the Age of Mechanical Reproduction," 414–29.

17. Barthes, "Camera Lucida." Ibid., 78.

18. Ibid., 81.

19. Ibid., 80.

20. Ibid., 49.

21. Ibid., 77.

22. Brainyquote, s.v. "Andy Warhol," http://www.brainyquote.com/quotes/authors/a/andy_warhol.html.

23. Mary Karr, *The Art of the Memoir* (New York: HarperCollins, 2015), 49.

24. David Foster Wallace, "Laughing with Kafka," *Harper's Magazine*, July 1998, 23.

25. Søren Kierkegaard, *The Sickness Unto Death: A Christian Psychological Exposition for Upbuilding and Awakening*, trans. Howard V. Hong and Edna H. Hong (Princeton, NJ: Princeton University Press, 1983), 68.

26. Ibid., 73.

27. Marc Maron Interviews Terry Gross, Letterman's Producer." *Fresh Air Weekend*. NPR. May 23, 2015, http://www.npr.org/2015/05/23/408773680/fresh-air-weekend-marc-maron-interviews-terry-gross-lettermans-producer.

28. Christian Wiman, *My Bright Abyss: Meditation of a Modern Believer* (New York: Farrar, Straus and Giroux, 2014), 9–10.

29. Ibid., 84.

30. Ibid., 111.

31. Steve Greene, "The 10 Best Films of 2015 So Far According to the Criticwire Network, Plus 40 More," *Criticwire*, Indiewire, June 17, 2015, http://blogs.indiewire.com/criticwire/the-10-best-films-of-2015-so-far-according-to-the-criticwire-network-plus-40-more-20150617. Sam Adams, "Criticwire Survey: What Indiewire's Critics Poll Gets Wrong About the Best Movies of 2015 So Far," *Criticwire*, Indiewire, June 23, 2015, http://blogs.indiewire.com/criticwire/criticwire-survey-what-indiewires-critics-poll-gets-wrong-about-the-best-movies-of-2015-so-far-20150623.

32. Alissa Wilkinson, "In Praise of Slow Opinions," *Christianity Today*, February 12, 2015, http://www.christianitytoday.com/ct/2015/february-web -only/in-praise-of-slow-opinions.html.

33. Mark O'Connell, "It's Comments All the Way Down," *The New Yorker*, June 17, 2015, http://www.newyorker.com/culture/cultural-comment/its -comments-all-the-way-down.

34. A. O. Scott, "Adjusting to a World That Won't Laugh With You," *The New York Times*, June 5, 2015, http://www.nytimes.com/2015/06/07/movies /adjusting-to-a-world-that-wont-laugh-with-you.html.

35. Ibid.

36. Louis C. K. "Louis C.K. On Life And Stand-Up: 'I Live In Service For My Kids.'" *Fresh Air with Terry Gross*. NPR. April 28, 2015, http://www .npr.org/programs/fresh-air/2015/04/28/402832708/fresh-air-for-april -28-2015.

37. Zadie Smith, "Man vs. Corpse," *The New York Review of Books*, December 5, 2013, http://www.nybooks.com/articles/2013/12/05/zadie-smith -man-vs-corpse.

38. "Giulianna Bruno," interview by Sarah Oppenheimer, *BOMB Magazine*, Summer 2014, http://bombmagazine.org/article/10056/giuliana -bruno. All quotations from Bruno in the following passages are taken from this interview.

39. Dennis Lim, "Wes Anderson's 'Moonrise Kingdom' with Bill Murray," *The New York Times*, May 11, 2012, http://www.nytimes.com/2012/05/13 /movies/wes-andersons-moonrise-kingdom-with-bill-murray.html.

40. Miriam Bratu Hansen, *Cinema and Experience: Siegfried Kracauer, Walter Benjamin, and Theodor W. Adorno*, ed. Edward Dimendberg (Berkeley, CA: University of California Press, 2011), 12.

41. Manohla Dargis, "'Spring Breakers,' Directed by Harmony Korine," *The New York Times*, March 14, 2013, http://www.nytimes.com/2013/03/15 /movies/spring-breakers-directed-by-harmony-korine.html.

42. Philip Larkin, "Water," *Collected Poems*, ed. Anthony Thwaite (New York: Farrar, Straus and Giroux, 2004).

43. Susan Sontag, "Notes on Camp," *Against Interpretation: And Other Essays* (New York: Picador, 2001), 282.

44. Ibid.

45. C. S. Lewis, *The Screwtape Letters* (New York: Touchstone Books, 1996), 7.

46. David Foster Wallace, *This Is Water: Some Thoughts, Delivered on a Significant Occasion, about Living a Compassionate Life* (New York: Little, Brown, 2009), 3–4.

47. Wiman, *My Bright Abyss*, 9.

48. Zadie Smith, interview by Christopher Bollen, *Interview Magazine*, September 4, 2012, http://www.interviewmagazine.com/culture/zadie-smith/.

49. Martin Heidegger, "The Question Concerning Technology," *Basic Writings*, rev. ed. (New York: HarperCollins, 1993), 311–41.

50. Lauren Winner, *Still: Notes on a Mid-faith Crisis* (New York: HarperOne, 2013), 41.

51. Zadie Smith, *On Beauty* (New York: Penguin Books, 2006), 286–87.

52. Maria A. G. Witek et al., "Syncopation, Body-Movement and Pleasure in Groove Music," *PLOS One* (April 2014), http://journals.plos.org/plosone/article?id=10.1371/journal.pone.0094446.

53. Michaeleen Doucleff, "Anatomy Of A Dance Hit: Why We Love To Boogie With Pharrell," NPR News, 2014, http://www.npr.org/sections/health-shots/2014/05/30/317019212/anatomy-of-a-dance-hit-why-we-love-to-boogie-with-pharrell.

54. Paul Tillich, *Systematic Theology,* vol. 3 (Chicago: The University of Chicago Press, 1963), 120–23.

55. Nancy Jo Sales, "Tinder and the Dawn of the 'Dating Apocalypse,'" *Vanity Fair*, August 6, 2015, http://www.vanityfair.com/culture/2015/08/tinder-hook-up-culture-end-of-dating.

56. Bruno, *BOMB* interview.

57. Zadie Smith, "Find Your Beach," *The New York Review of Books*, October 23, 2014, http://www.nybooks.com/articles/archives/2014/oct/23/find-your-beach/.

58. Valeriya Safronova, "Exes Explain Ghosting, the Ultimate Silent Treatment," *The New York Times*, June 26, 2015, http://www.nytimes.com/2015/06/26/fashion/exes-explain-ghosting-the-ultimate-silenttreatment.html.

59. Christian Wiman, "Kill the Creature," *The American Scholar*, Spring 2015, https://theamericanscholar.org/kill-the-creature.

60. Marcus Goodyear, "Digital Relationships Just Aren't as Powerful as Flesh and Blood," *The High Calling*, August 2, 2015, http://www.thehighcalling.org/articles/essay/digital-relationships-just-arent-powerful-flesh-and-blood.

61. Friedrich Kittler, "Towards an Ontology of Media," *Theory, Culture & Society* 26 (2009), 23–31.